the hiking-
climbing handbook

(Swiss National Tourist Office)

the hiking-climbing handbook

by curtis casewit

Hawthorn Books, Inc. Publishers New York

Other books by the same author:

THE BEATTIE LEARN TO SKI BOOK

HOW TO GET A JOB OVERSEAS

THE MOUNTAINEERING HANDBOOK

SKI FEVER

SKI RACING: ADVICE BY THE EXPERTS

acknowledgments

Many fellow hikers and climbers helped me with this book. I want to thank G. B. Lloyd, Jr., and K. Hinton, of the U.S. Forest Service; David Brower and Henry Mandolf, Sierra Club; Jim Kack, Holubar Mountaineering Ltd.; Yvon Chouinard and Tom Frost, piton specialists; and Gerry Cunningham, Colorado Outdoor Sports. Esther McDowell, my typist, was as speedy and accurate as always.

C. C.
Denver, Colorado

contents

introduction

Perhaps no endeavor in the world tests a man the way that mountain climbing does. It is a challenge to him mentally, emotionally, and physically. Yet despite the exhausting rigors of the climb, or maybe because of them, it offers an unmatched exhilaration. I don't know of anything that can match the sheer joy of standing on the top of a peak, looking out over a tremendous vista and thinking to yourself, "I made it."

It isn't so much that you have beaten the mountain, because that is still there, and will be always, but that you have mastered yourself. You have overcome weariness, fear, and self-doubt. Realizing this is about as much reward as a man can ask for.

People still ask, "Why do men climb mountains?" There are many answers, but Curtis Casewit gives one as good as any when he says, "The essence of it all is the experience you derive. Here you can discover a renewal of something within you. Call it an aloneness, a detachment from normal cares and responsibilities, or a feeling of your place in nature."

The best part of all this is that you don't have to climb a Himalayan peak to get this kind of feeling. You can do it on a Sunday-afternoon hike up a relatively small hill. As long as it tests your mettle, you'll get the feeling. Of course, the more experienced you become the tougher climbs you'll attempt and the deeper the feeling of accomplishment.

I'll go a step further and say that you don't have to reach the top at all to get a feeling of elation. No mountain is a single peak; it is many peaks, and there is a thrill of achievement in conquering each pitch.

This book will give you the groundwork for that experience. In it, Curtis Casewit gives you all of the information you'll need to begin climbing. He covers training, the proper clothing, shoes, and equipment, belaying, rappelling, ropes and pitons, and really practical advice on tents, sleeping bags, and packs.

But he gives a good deal more than that, too. He shows the techniques of rock climbing, thoroughly covers the important subject of what makes a good climber, and most important of all, drives home the lesson of safety. All of this learning, of course, should be done under the watchful eye of a good instructor at the beginning. The picture selection is excellent and does a fine job of illustrating all of the points brought out in the text. The author's obvious familiarity with good hiking and climbing areas throughout the country makes me envious, and I hope someday to get a chance to see more of them.

I like this book very much; I wish I could have had a copy years ago when I first started climbing. It would have saved me a good bit of trial and error. It is a book that should be read and re-read, not only by beginners but by the experienced climber as well—we can all do with a refresher course now and then.

I can heartily recommend this book for anyone interested in enjoying the rewards of hiking and climbing. If this becomes your passion, perhaps one day you will have the supreme moment I once had of standing at the top of the world.

James W. Whittaker
Seattle, Washington
July, 1969

1 go! all about hiking

Dawn. You set out. Across a meadow, then into a forest, still dark and mysterious at this hour. Pine needles muffle the sound of your steps. You breathe deeply: grasses, ferns, the bark of spruces. The trail now turns upward, becoming a staircase of rocks. Steeper and steeper. A sun-drenched ridge. The breeze touches your nostrils, cools your brow, stirs your mind. You're alive and feel your body. You have space.

You allow yourself a standing pause. The highway you left is already a silver wire far beneath you. Toy-size cars streak along down there. You don't envy the drivers, all cooped up while you're free to move. "Let's go!"

This is hiking.

You can do it in the mountains, in the hills, in the flatlands. Plato hiked through the olive groves of Greece. Emerson and Thoreau and Muir walked through our woods. John Kennedy liked the dunes of the seashore. And you? Wherever you go, set yourself a purpose! You may want to hike because you like to identify rocks or wild flowers, to watch the birds, to chase butterflies, or to see the leaves turn. Scenery alone makes hiking worth the effort for some people; for others it's just a fringe benefit.

Your best hikes are those with goals: a special lake where

the trout are jumping, a fire tower which affords the best view, or a famous waterfall. (You'll find many specific suggestions in chapters 3 and 4.)

Whatever your destination, hiking will charge up your batteries. To your astonishment, your mind becomes a gurgling fountain of ideas. Walking is magic. If you have problems, each step seems to bring you closer to a solution. Or if you wish, you can touch a mental button, and the problem vanishes. Gratefully, you keep in motion. It will make you feel good, better than you have felt in a long time. The fresh air lets your lungs work as they should. You drink and water never tasted so sweet. You eat with real appetite.

You can hike all morning without strain. On the contrary, you seem to get fresher, stronger, more alive.

It's necessary that you lay the groundwork for this enjoyment, though. First of all, try to walk as much as possible in your regular routine. Don't let anyone drive you to school —even if it rains! If you haven't hiked in mountain country before, start with short hikes of an hour or two. Get into condition. If you avoid steep terrain, you should be able to do two to three miles per hour. After a while, you'll do four miles per hour with ease. An experienced hiker will have no trouble with a twenty-mile hike in a day. (If you're interested in longer hikes, you'll find suggestions in Chapter 2.)

Remember that each trail—even in fairly flat country—is different and offers a unique experience. A particular trail may have scenery, historic features, or geological formations not duplicated on any other trail. Each trail is worth hiking and no two are alike.

Eventually you may want to work up to something like the two-thousand-mile Appalachian Trail! That's the longest marked trail in the world, even beating Alpine paths. This hiker's dream extends from Mount Katahdin, Maine, to Springer Mountain, Georgia, passing through thirteen states —Maine, New Hampshire, Vermont, Massachusetts, Connecticut, New York, New Jersey, Pennsylvania, Maryland,

YOUR BOOTS should fit well, or you may get blisters. A specialized store has a large selection and will let you try boots on with several pairs of socks. (*P. H. Schmuck*)

Virginia, Tennessee, North Carolina, and Georgia. Other hiking enthusiasts have tramped all the way from the Cascades through the Sierras to Mexico.

Yet such extremes are unnecessary at first. Try a hike of only a few miles, along the nearest river, or up the hills just outside your town.

What should you take along? On one-day trips this is fairly simple. You will need a light lunch (compactly wrapped) and a canteen or plastic (or aluminum) bottle of drinking water. Sunglasses and sun cream are good in the mountains. Camera, binoculars, small first-aid kit, whistle, compass, map, matches, knife, pencil and notebook are optional. A knapsack provides the most convenient means to carry what you need.

Trail hiking is also made more comfortable by the proper choice of footwear. What's proper? First of all, forget all about street shoes. Leather soles make poor contact with rocky surfaces, and you're likely to slip and fall. Tennis shoes or sneakers are all right for hiking a few miles on *dry* ground. For the mountains, however, tennis shoes are inadequate. They get wet. They offer little support for your ankle and little protection against bruises. And on long hill trips, sneakers do not give enough support to your arches. Real boots are better, especially if they come with lug soles. Boots should be sturdy, yet not too heavy. They need not cost more than twenty-five to thirty-five dollars. If you choose a laceable pair with (rubber-base) Vibram soles, you can use the same pair for rock climbing. (A specialized mountaineering store can help with the selection.) Climbing boots—and this includes the extra-light ones—should be very snug. Hiking boots, though, may be better if they allow room for two pairs of socks. (If your feet are still growing, you can later wear them with just a single pair.) If your boots are too tight, your toes will be squashed. That's painful when hiking downhill. You can get blisters from boots that are much too big or much too small. Break your boots in by walking in them at home, or by first wearing them on a two-mile hike.

An expert trail hiker advises, "A hiker must be foot-happy. You'll be doing plenty of footwork and for this reason sturdy, comfortable hiking boots are essential. These should be large enough, for added hiking comfort, to accommodate the necessary pairs of socks. Good, heavy wool socks and the addition of plastic mesh insoles that allow ventilation under the soles of the feet are the best combination for most purposes. Felt insoles will actually give more insulation than mesh insoles. But a dry pair must be carried, because once loaded with moisture, felt insoles become excellent conductors of heat. Your leather boots should be kept waterproof with a wax-type compound. Otherwise greases and oils soak into the leather and reduce its natural insulating properties. Loafers, sneakers, or moccasins are a welcome change in the evening after heavy boots on the trail."

Even on two-mile hikes, you should pay attention to your pace. You tire the least by keeping your pace consistent. Stick to one slow rhythm. Running and then slowing down won't do it. Crawling along and then speeding up won't do it. An erratic hike will quickly leave you breathless. An even tempo will get you anywhere you want to go with a minimum of fatigue.

Gung-ho madness, which is sometimes encountered in large groups, is dead-wrong. If you're in company, no one in the rear should have to run. And nobody up front should have to be impatient. This is especially important if you have a small sister or brother in tow.

The right tempo? You can do about three miles per hour on the flat ground. But when your trail goes *upward*, you'll have to deduct one mile per thousand feet of altitude. So in

RUNNING UPHILL like
this may seem like fun,
but it will tire you
very quickly. A steady
pace is preferred by
experienced hikers.
(*Union Pacific*)

THESE HIKERS are
understandably tired
after a long ascent.
They will be even more
exhausted when they
get up again.
It's an important
hiking rule to rest
while standing.
(*University of Colorado*)

the mountains you can only expect a trail speed of two miles an hour. Anything faster is, foolhardy.

Sprinting in the mountains doesn't pay. One summer, for instance, a top high school athlete tried it on Mount Rainier, Washington. He thought the guide was too slow so he dashed ahead of the much older man. An hour later he was burned out. As he stood gasping, trembling, and then coughing, he was soon overtaken by the guide. Racing uphill overworks the heart and lungs, and not even an Olympic track team trains that way. They never *run up*.

A slow pace when you begin to hike also means fewer stops. Have you ever noticed what happens when someone stops a heated car and then tries to start it again? It will start but not always easily. Your body reacts the same way. You should therefore try to limit halts. Some hikers avoid them altogether. Pause for a *brief* rest once an hour, or if you're really tired, every half hour. If you eat at this time, eat lightly. And don't sit down! This destroys rhythm, upsets your circulation, and stiffens your muscles. Lean against a tree or a rock, Stand up! (A few people have the theory that you ought to *lie* down and put your feet up high. Experts disagree.) The rest periods are for a drink of water (slowly, please) and for a talk with fellow hikers. When you get going again, talk should be kept to a minimum. You need your lungs for other labor.

While in motion, it's best not to get too hot. Maintain climate control. Avoid a lot of sweating. You do this by shedding some outer garments like parkas and jackets as you heat up. Then when it gets cold, or when you make another stop, you can put them on again. "The best way to stay warm is not to get hot," goes the hiker's credo, and it's true enough. Avoid hiking during the noonday heat!

Hiking is usually easiest in a group, under good leadership. Who is the leader? It could be you, if you have younger

WHETHER YOU HIKE with your family, with the
Boy Scouts, or with any other group, there
should always be a leader. He (or she) is
responsible for your safety. (*Swiss National Tourist Office*)

family members along, and have hiked before. It could be your father or a relative. It could be a scout troop chief. It could be an experienced friend. The good leader will not only set the right pace; he'll also set the right example by placing his feet carefully on the ground. He'll avoid loose rocks and logs. He won't step on wiggly boulders. If there's a mountain trail up a crest, he'll be careful to stay in the center. He'll guide you so well that you enjoy every step.

Even the most excellent leaders depend on the cooperation of the whole group. In one Western hiking group, for instance, a woman who led many people every week observed, "More often than should happen, people wander from the group without permission or even the knowledge of their leader. A later nose count reveals that perhaps two or three persons are missing. It then develops that Bill and his buddy just ducked out to explore a cave or perhaps to climb a rock spire they had spotted on the next ridge. The leader must now wait for them while the rest of the party fends for itself. Perhaps the wanderers don't take quite the same route back —and they miss the group. How does the trip leader know that the strays are back down at the cars while he still is up checking the ridge?

"Then there are always the few who rush on ahead of the slower group. Their main purpose in life is to race as fast as possible—for them. Guests or inexperienced climbers then think they too must keep up. As a result, the club members who tried to cooperate get tired, discouraged, and sometimes don't reach the trip's goal. It also spreads the party all over the mountain.

"Why should a member of the group let the leader know where he intends to go if he simply must leave the group? It's only common courtesy and it gives a vital safety margin as well. The leader might know that the innocent cave the member wants to explore hides a mine shaft with a five-hundred-foot vertical drop back in the shadows—or the leader's map may show his rock spire to be four miles away. If he doesn't want anyone to leave the party, the person can always get up a group of his own another day to come back and explore if he must."

Hiking—especially in the wilderness—becomes safest with at least two other people along. In case of an accident, you thus have someone to send for help. Many experts recommend groups of four and up. If you attempt a difficult hiking ascent, you might let a friend or a family member know where you're going. In the national parks, you can sign out at a ranger station. When you get back, you sign in. In our national parks and in state parks, it's always best to stick to the trails. If you go off-trail and try to find shortcuts, you're causing soil erosion. But on other mountainous or hilly terrain, there may be occasions when the trail leads only partway toward your objective. You will then have to leave the trail and travel cross-country.

Near the water, you'll find willows and other brush. If there are no trails, you'll find progress difficult and tiresome. Experienced hikers avoid what they call "bushwhacking," which means crossing a jungle of thick brush. Of course, in mountainous country, hard snow may cover the brush even through spring, and it won't be a problem to make your way over the hard surface. In the mountains, you can further avoid bushwhacking by going up windswept ridges. These are usually bare of snow. If you're lucky, there will be many large rocks in brush areas. These rocks allow better progress than battling the brush. Naturally, game trails through the bushes are always best, or you can utilize dry stream beds. Sometimes you have no choice but to bushwhack. If so, make sure that all equipment and loose items of clothing are well tied to you and thus can't be lost. In fact, you don't want to get lost yourself in such terrain. Always keep a companion in sight!

IF A RIVER is too deep or too swift, you may need a rope bridge to get across. It takes experts to rig up ropes for such crossings. Do not attempt it before learning how from a pro! (*Colorado Outward Bound School*)

At lower elevations, you may have to cross small rivers. Look for logs or stepping-stones. No easy route? You can then usually wade across. In some cases you may even have to go in over your knees or waist. When this happens, and particularly when the current is swift, use a rope for safety. A capable leader will take the rope across to the other bank and fasten the rope end to a strong tree or rock. Then the rest of the team can follow. Try to keep the pack dry. Secure your camera and any loose equipment.

Remember too that on some slopes, loose sand and small rocks often collect. These "scree" and sand slopes, although not dangerous, are difficult to climb because your feet slip before they eventually hold. Effort has to be duplicated in ascent, but they offer an ideal route of descent.

Keep in mind that mountain outings can bring some dangers. One of the serious ones: falling rock. Up or down, it's always safest to pick a zigzag route, so that no one in the party is in the path of cascading stone debris from the other people. And it's taboo to hurl rocks. Every summer hikers and climbers are badly hurt when exuberant youngsters bombard them without knowing it.

It's also wise to get used to the altitude before you strike out on a big hike. A few do-nothing days in the lodge or at camp are advisable. If you try a strenuous hike on your first mountain day, the thin air could make you dizzy and ill, especially if you try to go too fast.

Restraint is especially important for the flatlander while he is getting used to the altitude. They still talk about the Connecticut girl who laughed at the advice of a Colorado mountain club group. "What a bunch of slowpokes you are!" she told them. So she darted up Longs Peak. Above timberline, her strength petered out. She was washed up. Altitude sickness. She could have avoided it if she'd gone slowly and first spent a few days in the region. The precaution of getting used to elevation is particularly important in the Canadian Rockies, the Rocky Mountains of the Western U.S., the Cascades of the Northwest, and other high regions.

The wrong clothing can also mean a peril. Mountain weather is fickle; it can change every five minutes. Even in midsummer, hikers have frozen to death in New Hampshire because they set out in just a pair of shorts and a short-sleeved shirt. Be aware of weather conditions. Passes of eleven to twelve thousand feet can be stormy any time of year.

If you venture into especially cold country, here are the cardinal rules:

- Put on several layers of clothing.
- Keep your torso warm so it can send its excess heat to your less well insulated extremities.
- Keep wind and rain out of your insulation by suitable outer covering or protection.
- If your feet are cold, put your hat on. That may sound funny, but those who understand how the human body works know it is a fact. So use your head. Keeping it covered helps force heat to your extremities. Uncovering it early avoids sweating.

In many places it is impossible to forecast the temperatures you may encounter. In the Canadian province of Alberta, for instance, the days may be hot and the nights extremely chilly. On a clear, sunny day the mercury may climb to the high seventies; evening may find it plunging to the low forties. Not only temperature changes but also an occasional rain or snow shower can enliven the hikers' day. An official of the "Skyline Trail Hikers of the Canadian Rockies" therefore suggests: "Bring a warm jacket, sweater or blanket coat and a raincoat or slicker (light in weight) to carry on the trail. A shirt of wool or other warm material is the most

A PAIR OF LONG SLACKS would be better than shorts. Knees get scraped when you climb in shorts, and mountain weather is capricious. Several layers of clothing are your best insulation against the possible onset of bad weather. (*N.Y. Dept. of Commerce*)

comfortable and serviceable item of apparel; checks, plaids and bright colors are favored. Slacks, pedal pushers, blue jeans are very popular with hikers. A hat which will give protection to the nose, face and head is particularly important."

There are other points to learn. As you read further, you'll find out how not to get lost (and what to do if you are), and about taking longer and more challenging trips.

But don't let dangers and challenges frighten you. In the end you'll find that hills and mountains are marvelous to you. Hiking becomes a lifetime habit, helping you keep your health and your mental balance thanks to physical balance, giving you pride and a glow of achievement. Why should you try it? An official of the Colorado Outdoor Sports Corporation gives some of the best reasons. Says Gerry Cunningham, "Trail bikes are found deep in the forest where foot traffic is much more appropriate. In winter, snow machines carry people who should be skiing or snowshoeing. People will haul a six-hundred-pound fully loaded motorboat over a mile-long portage to avoid paddling a canoe. Half the exercise has even gone out of a game of golf for those who ride around the course in an electric buggy. All in all it is hard to see how this laziness can benefit the health of our nation. A man should take pride in the distance he can walk, not in how far he can force his jeep past the end of the road.

"To escape from the noise and smell of motor vehicles is to shed half the pressure of modern life. To travel through an unspoiled countryside under one's own power and at one's own pace is to return for a moment to the serenity of nature. Walking is the basic form of natural travel."

So it's all there for you, waiting.

A HIKE IS THE best way to escape from
our motorized world. (*Colorado Outward Bound School*)

2 go far: backpacking

Backpacking is just hiking longer distances for longer periods. In other words, backpacking is advanced hiking. Some people also call it "knapsacking." Thanks to campcraft, backpacking will take you places no other transportation can go. It certainly will give you the chance to break away from the permanent campfire grates and heavy rustic tables of the campground, venture into wilderness country with your home on your back, and know the joys of stopping when and where you will without thinking about schedules or definite destinations.

Backpacking offers freedom found in no other type of wilderness travel. No worry about tying up the horse when you pause to brew a cup of tea or swim in a mountain stream. No wondering if you can pick your way over the rocks or across the snowfield. No searching for pasture when it is time to make camp or carrying oats to supplement natural feed. Self-sufficient, you need consider only the whims and comforts of your friends and yourself.

Requirements? Don't try backpacking if you haven't hiked before. You need physical stamina; and if you sit in front of a television set every night, eating popcorn balls, and never do any exercise you'll be in no shape for a long trail.

WHILE CHAIR-LIFT RIDERS can only reach one part
of the mountain, the backpackers can go anywhere,
for any length of time. (*Swiss National Tourist Office*)

According to the Sierra Club, which organizes many trips
for younger people, "the knapsacker doesn't have to be a
robust fellow with a broad back and bulging calf, who
charges up the ridges without a pause." It could also be the
wiry young man—or girl—hiking a trail deliberately. You
don't have to be a superman. You merely have to be healthy,
in shape, and able to carry your own gear. "You don't just *go*
backpacking, you *prepare* for it," is one Sierra Club slogan.
This takes conditioning, especially for the higher altitudes. If
you're a beginner, start with a trial run. Make it short and on
level ground. Get your muscles toned up. See if the isolated
backcountry agrees with you. Get the feel of your pack.

With enough training, anyone can take long weekend trips. The U.S. Forest Service files contain many stories to prove this. In Washington State, for example, three-year-old Kathie hiked 4½ miles into wilderness in the Wenatchee National Forest where her folks were going to camp a week. It took her six hours, not because she got tired, but because she found so many fascinating things to examine on the way. And four children, ages five, seven, eight, and nine, hiked fourteen miles to a wilderness camp spot in the Bridger National Forest, Wyoming. When a forest ranger met the tired youngsters, they were grinning from ear to ear, proud that they had packed in their own gear.

You must be smart in your choice of gear. Listen to this good advice from the famous Sierra Club:

> • Do not rush into procuring all equipment at once.
> • Observe what others are using and ask why. More experienced mountaineers have definite opinions as to why they prefer one form of equipment to another. Climbers' opinions will aid you in forming your own opinion and evaluating sales claims.
> • Set up a priority list of essential equipment. Some items will probably have to be military surplus, for a while, in order to keep the original cost within your budget.

And the Colorado Mountain Club suggests that members ask themselves these questions: "When buying equipment, consider:

> Will it do what I expect it to?
> Will it last with hard wear?
> Do I really need it?

And beware of the salesman's advice—he may never have had any backpacking experience."

If you go on a backpacking trip for a whole week, you may wish to study this suggested checklist by the Alpine Club of Canada:

Essential Items

Ground sheet
Warm sleeping bag
Tent
Pack
Sunglasses
Plastic or metal cup
Flashlight with extra batteries
Boots with Vibram soles *and extra laces*
Waterproofing for boots
Jeans or knickers
Warm underwear—a change
3 or 4 shirts with long sleeves
2 complete sock changes–4 pairs minimum
2 pairs of gloves or mitts–1 wool
2 warm sweaters
Windproof jacket (preferably ¾-length with hood)
Wool cap or toque
Hat with brim or peak
Coat or wrap for campfires
Towel
Soap
Toothbrush and paste
Handkerchiefs
Darning and mending material
Sunburn cream
Insect-repellent stick or liquid
Lip ointment
Pair of shoes for use around camps
Spare pants
Cooking equipment: plates, fork, knife, spoon

Optional Items

Air mattress or polyurethane pad
Camera and film
Liner for sleeping bag
Cord for clothesline, clothespins
Reading matter
Scarf
Bathing suit or sunsuit
Matches in waterproof case
Polyethylene water bottle
Good pocket knife

The most important purchases are your pack, sleeping bag, and tent. Let's take a look at these items, one by one. Since backpacking involves staying overnight, we will begin with tents.

SPECIALIZED mountaineering stores
such as this one contain large assortments
of all necessary items. (*James W. Whittaker*)

Tents

Must you really have a tent? In some regions, summer rain is rare and tents are not necessary. One of the nicest spots to sleep in such country is on a rocky ledge that holds the heat of the afternoon sun far into the night and gives protection from wind. An overhanging branch will provide a natural roof with clothes hooks. Avoid, however, camping under dead branches, near leaning trees, or in the path of rock slides.

You can bring a shelter other than a tent. In mild climates, a nylon ground cloth or a large piece of plastic at least nine by twelve feet, preferably with grommets along the sides, can be tied up to trees to keep you dry. Some people use their ponchos for this purpose. There are numerous ways to fix such shelters. String a rope from one tree to another. Throw the plastic over the rope and attach the corners to other trees, one end lower than the other. Under this roof you can prepare meals in case of rain and three or four people can sleep. One-man shelter? Put part of the ground cloth on the ground as a protection for your air mattress. Then run the ground cloth on a slant over the air mattress and hitch to overhanging branches, thus forming a V where you sleep. If the open end of the V is up against a big log, you have a snug little nest into which to crawl for the night.

In some places you can also eliminate the tent by using three-sided trail shelters, which have been built along many trails for the convenience of hikers. These shelters follow a general pattern. A slightly raised sleeping platform in the rear can accommodate from eight to a dozen people, depending on the size of the shelter and the people. In front is usually a firepit with a large back rock to reflect the heat of the fire into the shelter. Remember that shelters are occupied on a first-come, first-served basis. Latecomers rig up a shelter outside.

IN SOME CLIMATES a tent may not be necessary,
and you do not need the most expensive tent
when you do acquire one. (*Colorado Outdoor Sports Corp.*)

ON SOME HIKES a cave can be found for
rest or sleep. (*Boulder Chamber of Commerce*)

All this can make backpacking very inexpensive. On the other hand, you may have no choice but to carry a tent in the high mountains or in rainy regions. How much should you spend? A tent can cost anywhere from five to two hundred dollars. On the average, you'll spend about fifty dollars. Certainly, the most expensive tents are not always the best. You may be better off with a simple army tent than the ritziest, most advertised, most gimmicky $200 job. A mountaineer who spent several summers in one of the West's Outward Bound Climbing Camps as an instructor roamed the Rockies with just a military tent. As a storm started brewing on a crest, a couple of other campers arrived with a well-advertised hexagonal miracle. By midnight the wind started blowing in earnest; at dawn, the winds reached fifty miles per hour. The instructor's army tent shook and trembled and made tortured noises under the evil sky. For a full day, the driving rain continued. The wind still didn't cease at night. Finally, the second morning, the men could venture outside. The military tent hadn't budged in the deluge; the expensive tent had been ripped up and swept downhill, where the other backpackers now picked up the tattered remains. In the same vein, even an Everest tent—which is fine against falling snow, blizzards, and cold spells—won't do you much good at the low, wet elevations. (Here only waterproofing counts, and this includes a waterproof floor.) A tent should be light, of course—especially when *you* have to be the burro that trots it to the high mountain camp. But for low-level camping, weight doesn't matter so much, and the windproofing factors aren't critical either.

There are lightweight tents, designed for backpacking, that give a lot of protection. With a floor and a netting over the entrance they are insect-proof, animal-proof, and waterproof. Stakes slightly larger than a nail and lightweight telescopic aluminum poles rolled in the tent make a compact package.

MODERN TENTS are light, and easy to put up.
The system of stakes has been simplified
in recent years. (*Colorado Outdoor Sports Corp.*)

Tent materials present a problem, though. Breath condenses in some watertight nylon tents. This causes dampness. Waterproofed cotton, on the other hand, isn't completely watertight. Many backpackers get around this by using a cloth tent and stretching a nylon or plastic fly over it.

You can improve the situation by picking your campsite with care. A ravine could become a waterway in case of rain. Camping too close to a stream can mean flooding, and that murmuring brook can be a chilly neighbor. Yet when you make your site selection (and give yourself plenty of time) you ought to have drinking water close by. Dubious water should always be boiled in a pot or kettle. Remember, too, that you go upstream for your drinking supplies, and that you wash downstream.

When camping, look for level, rock-free ground, and be sure that there's fuel wood in the vicinity. Camp before darkness sets in; otherwise you may be too tired to eat, and need a lot of flashlight activity to stake the tent. Early camping also allows you to see the view and to observe the sunset. Pitch the tent where it gets morning sun, so it can dry out standing before it is packed. Note the wind direction in deciding which way to face. The wind will blow from a lake onto the shore and down a canyon at night; in reverse during the day.

Some young people can adjust their bones to the hard ground and still awake refreshed. On the other hand, equipment companies have come out with light and durable air mattresses for backpacking. Many backpackers use them. A mattress from the shoulders to just below the hips is all that you need for comfort. It is a good idea to put some gear under feet and legs for warmth.

Mattresses are made of plastic, nylon, or rubber. Your main consideration in selecting one is weight and durability. Most people blow up their air mattresses too much. A good test is to sit on the mattress. You should only slightly feel the

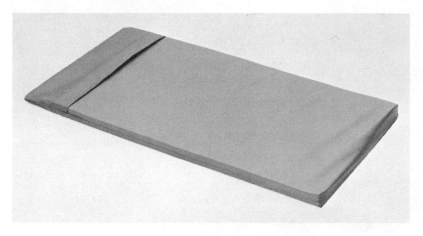

A FOAM PAD such as this one rolls up easily,
and gives you a good night's sleep. Many
backpackers prefer air mattresses. (*D. C. Saum*)

ground. Deflating the mattress? Simple. Before rising, take
out the plug or valve and let your body help push out the air.
Foam pads, which do not have to be inflated, have become
popular as mattresses, too.

Sleeping Bags

As a backpacker you'll also need a sleeping bag, or
"sleeper" for short. A whole book could be written on this
subject. Surely, a favorite indoor topic of conversation on a
long winter night is comparing the relative merits of the
many types on the market. A good rule to remember is: If a
bag is light and compact, it's a comfort to carry; if it's thick
and warm, it's a comfort to sleep in. Weight, warmth, and
shape are prime considerations.

Decide how much warmth you need and buy accordingly.
Look for stitching and shape in a bag. Stitching is needed to
prevent bunching of the filling, but it should not go through
the outer cloth of the sleeper.

Mummy bags, tapered at the foot, are popular, but they do
cut down foot room. Bags with zippers all the way down one
side and across the foot are easiest to get into and out of, and

HERE IS A down-filled, all nylon "mummy" sleeper. (*Colorado Outdoor Sports Corp.*)

IT'S NOT A bad idea to try your sleeping bag for size before buying it. (*Holubar Mountaineering, Ltd.*)

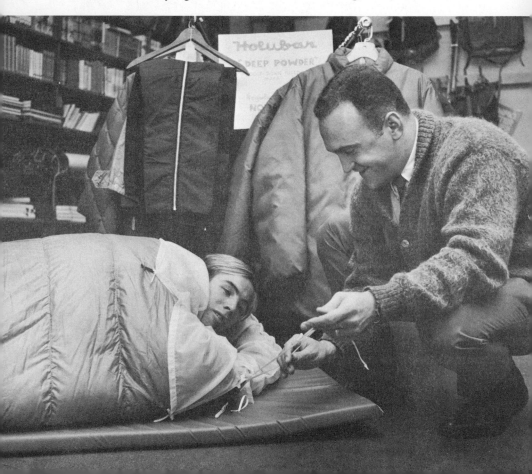

by unzipping a little or a lot you can regulate the warmth. These bags are usually rectangular in shape and can be spread out like a comforter. They're nice and roomy. Mummy bags come with a built-in hood for warmth. Others have a flap that reaches up over the head, providing shelter against rain and drafts. Head protection is necessary if you take no tent along. Drafts around the head and neck can be very chilling, even on a mild night, and if one part of the body is chilled, you get cold all over. Another sleeper is the blanket bag, which is not very compact, weighs more, and is not as warm. Kapok bags *are* warm, but often bulky. Dacron is liked by many people. Down bags are the lightest for the warmth provided and will roll up into a compact package easy to carry. They are also the most expensive.

Just what is down and where does it come from? Down is the insulation geese and other waterfowl have against the coldest weather. It is not a feather, but a central pod out of which dozens of filaments grow in all directions. It grows underneath the feather, next to the bird's skin. In its prime grades, goose down is the finest insulation known to man. Goose down has these advantages:

First, it is so lightweight that one ounce alone insulates about five hundred cubic inches. Second, goose down compresses easily; the same ounce that insulates five hundred cubic inches will compress under very little pressure to fifteen cubic inches. This not only means that sleeping bags will stuff into amazingly small sacks when not needed, but that two inches of goose down insulation is not as cumbersome and restrictive as the heavier insulations. Third, down lets the body moisture escape freely. Fourth, down is resilient, always coming back to its full size, while other materials fatigue quickly and lose their thickness.

Down sleeping bags are not inexpensive. You pay anywhere from $50 to $150 because down is so scarce. For some backpacking trips (in warm country, for instance) the advantages of a down sleeper are totally unnecessary and buying such a bag would be a waste of money.

If you've made the big investment, you may need some pointers on how to treat your down sleeping bag. A leading expert in outdoor research has this advice:

1. Fluff it up. Don't wait until you are ready for bed before pulling your sleeper out of its stuff sack. As soon as the tent is up, open out your sleeper and fluff it up. Fluff it up again before you crawl in.

2. Keep it loose. Try not to roll against the side of the tent, or allow packs or boots to lie on the sleeper. A good sleeper has enough down to keep itself at the proper thickness, but not enough to resist outside pressures. Lift your feet up and shake the bag so it puffs up just before you settle down, then pull the inside close to you to cut down the air space inside the bag to a minimum.

3. Insulate underneath. When your body compresses the down there is no thickness of insulation left. If you don't carry a foam pad or air mattress, put your clothing underneath your hips and shoulders and your feet up on your pack. Dry grass under the tent floor is also a help, and dry ground of any sort is warmer than damp ground. (This applies to every type of sleeping bag.)

4. Keep dry in all sleepers. Don't wear wet socks and clothing inside your bag. Wet or damp down will not fluff up, and its thickness is quickly lost. Air out every type of bag in warm sun, both right side and inside out, as often as possible. After a trip let your bag air out with occasional fluffing before storing. A bag is like a sponge. Squeeze the old air out and let fresh air in. Don't dry a nylon bag close to an open fire. Nylon melts at 482 degrees Fahrenheit and the radiant heat from glowing embers is enough to melt nylon if held too close.

5. Keep down bags clean. Dirt will destroy the fluff of down. A down sleeper may be dry-cleaned in a petroleum-base solvent, but it is better to wash it yourself. Wash it gently, in an automatic washer or by hand with detergent and warm water. Prescrub around the face opening or other heavily soiled areas. Spin-dry or gently squeeze all excess water out of the bag and then dry several cycles in an automatic drier. This will not entirely dry the bag. Spread it out on a bed in a warm room and shake and squeeze it several times a day until it is thoroughly dry and fluffy. Do not try to make the bag water-repellent by submerging it in a solution of repellent. This will adversely affect the down. Instead, spray the outside fabric only.

6. Keep yourself warm. Don't stand around in wet clothes getting thoroughly chilled and then expect to climb in the bag and warm right up. Put your extra clothing on before you get chilled.

7. When you go to bed eat a candy bar. The digestive process will help to warm you up. Also, if your clothes are not wet, try getting undressed inside the sleeping bag. By the time you get your pants and socks off inside a close-fitting bag you will have worked up quite a head of steam and be off to a good warm night's sleep.

Packs

Now that we have discussed tents and sleeping bags, let's consider packs. These come in all sizes, shapes, and price ranges. Each pack has its own purpose, and the one you choose depends on whether you'll be in the wilderness for only a few hours, for a full day, or a full week. Are you planning to carry a heavy load or a light one?

The simplest pack, called a "rucksack" or "knapsack," will serve you well on a half-day or full-day trail hike. You can easily load five to eight pounds into a rucksack. If you

A RUCKSACK like this
one works fine for
short trips, but if
you overload it, it
will pull you forward.
(*Colorado Outdoor
Sports Corp.*)

MODERN PACKS are
streamlined and smooth.
You can carry heavier
loads and still walk
straight. A few come
with frames.
(*Colorado Outdoor
Sports Corp.*)

MODERN PACKS like this one weigh as little as two pounds. There are separate compartments for various kinds of gear. (*Colorado Outdoor Sports Corp.*)

put too much weight into it, the sack will pull you forward. Moreover, heavier rucksacks are uncomfortable—the straps will bite into and rub against your shoulders. Remember, too, that a rucksack doesn't come with enough room for a standard sleeping bag, so you can't use this type of pack for overnight trips. Nor is the rucksack practical for rockclimbing, because the sack is too broad and awkward for maneuvering between close-together rock walls. Rucksacks are inexpensive, however, and ideal for short outings.

Your next choice is the oval-shaped, or tear-shaped, "contour" pack. This one also hugs your back, but it is much more streamlined. The pack has zippers instead of buckles, meaning that you won't get entangled in brush or between tight rocks. Such a pack is far lighter than a rucksack, too, and you can carry a load of ten to twenty pounds in it. There is room for a lightweight sleeping bag, so you can stay overnight, if necessary. A contour pack doesn't always come with a frame. The modern shape and material (generally nylon) brings the "contour" bag's cost up. Count on spending from ten to twenty dollars.

For longer hikes that require weights above twenty to twenty-five pounds, you will need *a pack with a frame*. The most popular frames are now made of tubular aluminum. Remember that a frame will hug your back, so that the pack will not swing off balance when you jump from rock to rock or hike along narrow ledges. And a frame (also called "packboard") makes for cool travel, since the pack attached to the frame never touches the body. Wooden frames will save you money, but they are uncomfortable. If you can't afford high prices, try finding low-cost aluminum frames in a surplus store.

You can mount on the frame a bag of your own selection. Prices for each vary from five to twenty-five dollars. A good pack should not weigh over six pounds empty. A waist strap will provide stability and support. Make sure that the pack fits you well, and holds all your gear.

You can make backpacking more comfortable by careful organization of your duffel. First of all, remember that your pack's outside pockets are handy for anything needed during the day. These pockets, and the outside of the pack, are the places for priority equipment like your maps, compass, rain parka, sweater, wool cap, gloves, lunch. Try to have heavy items, such as hardware, at the top of the pack and toward the inside, where they will carry better. The food goes inside, too. Keep it toward the top, and pretty well centered.

Food

How much food should you carry? Estimates vary from 1½ to 2½ pounds per day, according to U.S. Forest Service surveys. Much depends on the type of food you take along and on your hunger. But you can figure that exercise will

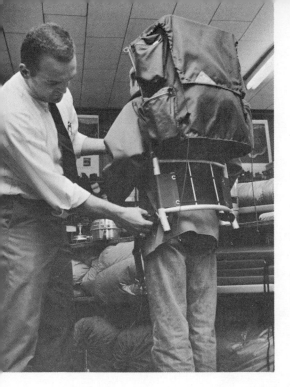

HERE'S THE IDEAL PACK for
a week-long trip, when you may
have to carry anywhere from
twenty to forty pounds of
food, cooking utensils,
tents, bags, and other items.
The aluminum frame allows
plenty of air between the
pack and your body.
Have yourself fitted by
an expert.
(*Holubar Mountaineering, Ltd.*)

A GOOD PACK FRAME
allows this girl to
carry heavy loads without
difficulties. Outside
pockets are handy for
frequently needed items.
(*U.S. Forest Service*)

increase your appetite. Food is the fuel that will keep your engine going. Hiking up a steep trail with a forty-pound pack on your back, you consume calories at a rate of five hundred to six hundred per hour. And you need a balanced diet of protein, fat, and carbohydrates to keep in top condition.

Keep in mind that cans are heavy, and so are glass jars. In the last few years, dehydrated food has improved both in taste and variety. Supermarkets carry instant rice, instant potatoes, instant puddings, and appetizing dried soups such as potato leek, mushroom, and tomato beef. Some stores stock fancy freeze-dried foods such as shrimp supreme, turkey Tetrazzini, and chicken stew. But you pay a high price for freeze-dried foods, especially if you go in for fancy dishes. On the other hand, companies selling to campers have developed simple meals such as beef and spuds, chicken and rice, beef and macaroni. They are continually adding to their vegetable line, and now it is possible to get dehydrated green salad. You can even get freeze-dried breakfast combinations—bacon and eggs or ham and eggs with fried potatoes.

Don't forget coffee and tea for an eye-opener and quick pickup. Instant cocoa tastes good in high country; and bouillon cubes not only make a good drink but a good flavoring for one-dish meals. Powdered milk is almost a must. Bread is optional. Carry a loaf, a can, or Scandinavian flatbrods, which are thin and light. Nuts, raisins, chocolate, and other candy are old standbys for backpackers. So is salami or dried beef. And taking along a few vitamin pills won't hurt, either.

Cooking Equipment

Keep cooking equipment simple. Most backpackers and hikers prefer a nesting of pots with covers, and a light frying pan. Take paper plates too. Don't forget waterproof matches, and some candles to make quicker fires when the wood is wet. Make sure to get a campfire permit before you leave. Most often, however, you're allowed to use fallen branches or dead trees as fuel. In national forest wilderness, such wood is usually plentiful. Canadians should inquire of forest authorities, and in some sections of the United States, like the southern Appalachians, it pays to take along a light-weight, one-burner gasoline stove. For chopping wood take an ax with at least a 2½- to 3-pound head and a 28- to 30-inch handle.

When building a fire, clear the ground of grass, leaves, and other flammable material. Circle the burning area with rocks, leaving cleared space outside the rocks. Keep water near in case the flames spread, especially if the ground is very dry. Most experienced campers keep their cooking fires small, concentrating the heat and at the same time saving wood.

When you break camp, make sure the fire is dead out. Dump water on the ashes; stir them in with the soil. Roll away stones from fireplaces, following the old adage "Where I go, I leave no sign."

3 locale:
hiking trails
(east and canada)

Where should you hike? North America is a vast continent, with trails in every state and Canadian province. And although the frontier has been pushed back, there is still much wilderness to roam and explore.

Hikers discover wilderness in many places and in many ways. For some it may be just a day's hike through the forested Linville Gorge in North Carolina, or a climb above timberline on Washington volcanoes. Others may roam remote mountains and lakes in the Bob Marshall Wilderness in Montana, or search for the famous Lost Dutchman Mine in the Superstition Mountain Wilderness of Arizona.

Remember that you do not need high mountains to find a path to suit you and the Southern states have many fine places for hikers. If you happen to be in Miami, Florida, for example, you have many walking possibilities in the Everglades National Park. The beaches of Alabama, Louisiana, and Texas offer opportunities for long hikes. Georgia has the Kennesaw Trail, and if you're in Gatlinburg, Tennessee, you should try a long nature exploration in the Great Smokies National Park. All over the U.S., the Sierra Club has fought for the continued existence of primitive regions. And often won.

NATIONAL FORESTS are found from coast to coast.
These hikers are making camp in the Mount Baker
National Forest, Washington State. (*U.S. Forest Service*)

Within some wilderness areas, you can still see whitetail, mule deer, elk, bighorn, mountain goat, peccary, and bear. For the scientist and nature student, the geology and ecology of each area can provide many hours of fascinating study. And for everyone there is solitude in the midst of unspoiled scenery. The essence of it all is the experience you derive. Here you can discover a renewal of something within you. Call it an aloneness, a detachment from normal cares and responsibilities, or a feeling of your place in nature.

Some of the best trails are in the national forests and national parks. In addition, there are state parks. Space? Our national forest system alone includes 154 national forests and 19 national grasslands, in forty-two states. These public lands are administered by the Forest Service, U.S. Department of Agriculture. The forests range in size from the 8.4-square-mile (5,400 acres) Great Gulf Wild Area in New Hampshire to the 1,240,000-acre Selway-Bitterroot Wilderness in Idaho and Montana, an area almost equal to the size of Delaware. In all, you have at your disposal 186,000,000 acres of these national forest lands! In addition, the National Park Service administers more than two hundred areas in the fifty states, Puerto Rico, and the Virgin Islands. Three categories are used to classify park installations: natural areas, historical areas, and recreational areas. Each year these national parks properties, covering some twenty-six million acres, are enjoyed by more and more people. Many of the trails in these areas are closed to motorized traffic.

Let's take a look at the locales and specific possibilities wherever you may live.

Let's begin in New York City. If you are a New Yorker, you have—despite all those stone buildings—many miles of waterfront greens and walking ways. Central Park and other city parks have extensive trail systems, including nature trails. Trails have been constructed along the great expressways and the extended Kissena Corridor. The location and length of the various trails can be found in a booklet issued by the New York City Department of Parks and Recreation entitled *Recreational Facilities for New Yorkers.*

If you live in New York State, you'll find many trails fanning out from the Lake Placid region. The Catskill Mountains are honeycombed with hiking paths, where you'll quickly forget the big resorts. Remember, too, that the Finger Lakes Trail stretches for more than one hundred miles from the Catskills to Allegheny State Park, connecting with pretty lakes and with the Bruce Trail in Canada. You can get information about the Finger Lakes Trail from the FLT Secretary, 2783 Brighton-Henrietta Town Line Road, Rochester, New York 14623.

A little farther west, you should consider the Baker Trail in Pennsylvania. With a length of 110 miles, it leads through farmland and woodland. It is well marked and has five shelters along the way. It starts at Freeport and runs north to Cook Forest State Park. For more information write to the Pittsburgh Council of American Youth Hostels, Inc., 6300 Fifth Avenue, Pittsburgh, Pennsylvania 15232.

Another useful lead for Pennsylvanians is the Horse-Shoe Trail Club, Inc., 1600 Three Penn Center Plaza, Philadelphia, Pennsylvania 19102. This fine group maintains the Horseshoe Trail. It begins at historic Valley Forge, Pennsylvania, and ambles along old roads and paths through beautiful country virtually free of motor traffic. At intervals along the trail are farmhouses where overnight lodging is offered to members of the American Youth Hostels, Inc.

The Horseshoe Trail follows high ridges and crosses many streams. It extends for 121 miles and joins the Appalachian Trail at Rattling Run Gap on Stoney Mountain twelve miles north of Hershey, Pennsylvania.

The Appalachian Trail, two thousand miles long, is America's super trail. It goes all the way from the Maine peaks down to Springer Mountain, Georgia. What an asset to the Eastern United States and to the South! The Appalachian Trail gives hikers a chance to see any or all of eight national forests, two national parks, scores of state forests and parks, and miles of private land. Foot travel for thirteen states! You can take an hour's walk, a full day's hike, or an extended outing (shelters provided). There are places where the novice can enjoy himself without losing track of familiar sights and sounds. There are mountains where only the experienced hiker should go.

Along the trail you can relax in the cool spruce and birch forests of New England. You can hike the steep trails in the White Mountain National Forest, cross the boulder-strewn range high above timberline, and skirt the Great Gulf Wild Area near Mount Washington.

In Vermont, after sweeping through the Connecticut River Valley and low hills, the trail joins the Long Trail at Route U.S. 4. From there it twists and turns along the backbone of the state—the Green Mountains in a national forest of the same name—to the Massachusetts line.

The Appalachian Trail has enormous variety. There are alpine tundra in New England; pastoral scenes in Vermont, Pennsylvania, and Virginia; areas containing timber for mills; lands rich in minerals; flora ranging from the Greenland sandwort of the north to the vivid flame azalea of the south; fauna from the bull moose to the short-tailed shrew. In Pennsylvania, which you know of already from the Horseshoe Trail, you traverse the old coal and iron country, through the St. Anthony's Wilderness where an old railroad grade, foundations of houses, and coal diggings are reminders that families lived here and a town flourished. West of the

Susquehanna you go through Mont Alto State Forest, site of one of the first forestry schools in the country.

At the Potomac River you parallel the old Chesapeake and Ohio Canal, an early transportation route between Cumberland, Maryland, and Alexandria, Virginia. You pass within sight of Harpers Ferry in West Virginia where abolitionist John Brown staged his pre–Civil War raid.

In the Shenandoah National Park the trail crisscrosses Skyline Drive for ninety-four miles. As it penetrates the George Washington National Forest in Virginia it becomes more remote and traverses a set of magnificent four-thousand-foot peaks. Through the Jefferson National Forest it runs across valleys and along ridges bearing such descriptive names as Angels Rest, Dragons Tooth, and Dismal Peak.

Throughout the southern Appalachians you see the trunks of the once great American chestnut trees which succumbed to blight. In this area, too, are the balds—rolling mountains with grassy tops, green and restful to a foot-weary traveler.

From here the trail winds over Roan Mountain on the boundary between the Pisgah National Forest in North Carolina and the Cherokee National Forest in Tennessee, where rhododendrons grow in great profusion. Through the Great Smoky Mountain National Park and into the Nantahala National Forest the trail continues, ending finally on Springer Mountain in the Chattahoochee National Forest, near Mount Oglethorpe, Georgia.

Back in New England, the northern terminus of the Appalachian Trail is 5,267-foot Mount Katahdin in Baxter State Park, Maine. From this point the trail winds southwesterly along the shores of numerous lakes and ponds, traversing wilderness terrain.

On the Appalachian Trail. (*U.S. Forest Service*)

On Mount Washington in New Hampshire, piles of rocks (called cairns) mark the trails. (*U.S. Forest Service*)

In New Hampshire, you enter the Presidential range, famous for its peaks above timberline and the Great Gulf Wilderness. Southwesterly in the White Mountain National Forest, you reach areas great in geological interest and scenic grandeur that have attracted hikers for generations.

For further information be sure to write to The Appalachian Trail Conference, 1718 North Street, N.W., Washington, D.C. 20036.

There are many other possibilities in New England. Consider, for example, Baxter State Park in Maine. Here you have eighty-three miles of trails, including the popular Hunt Trail which leads to Baxter Peak (elevation: 5,267 feet), the Marston Trail, Chimney Pond Trail, Northwest Basin Trail, Russell Pond Trail. Many of these can be easily done in a day. More ambitious hikers can tackle some of the forty-six mountain peaks in this park. The most exciting and the highest point in Maine is Mt. Katahdin. No nearby mountains challenge Katahdin in height or size. The park has log shelters for backpackers, campgrounds, and several fire lookouts.

The Long Trail starts at the Canadian border in Vermont and goes into Massachusetts. It is 255 miles long, including 80 miles in Green Mountain National Forest. The trail is well marked, and there are many shelters along the way. For information write to: The Green Mountain Club, Inc., 63 Center Street, Rutland, Vermont.

Farther north, in Quebec, the Laurentians (also called Laurentides) are crisscrossed by trails. You can get details from the Canadian Government Travel Bureau in Ottawa, Ontario. The province of Ontario is also rich in land for hikers. The Bruce Trail, for example, stretches some 480 miles from Queenston to Tobermory following the Niagara Escarpment. Some sections are well marked, have shelters, and remain close to civilization; others are very much in the wilderness and need maps. The trail also cuts through the

THE CANADIAN province of Alberta is honeycombed
by hiking trails. Note hikers' rucksacks for
one-day outings. (*Canadian Govt. Travel Bureau*)

most populated part of Ontario. But you rarely come within sight of modern civilization. At points along this scenic wonderland are campsites and chalet-style hostels.

The northern end of the Bruce is rugged and defiant. Crawl-and-slide is often necessary along the craggy Georgian Bay shore.

Another prime Ontario attraction is the Opeongo Line, a pioneer trail that crams one hundred years of history into one hundred miles of captivating countryside. Starting at Farrell's Landing on the Ottawa River, it runs northwesterly to its end at Lake Opeongo in Algonquin Provincial Park.

Gentle paths for outings lie within the very environs of most urban Ontario centers, including the provincial capital, Toronto.

The Canadian province of Nova Scotia has many trails through lake and forest country. Spring and summer are the best times to hike because there is no danger from hunters at that time. One well-known foot trip is a twelve-mile hike through the woods of Peggy's Grove past several lakes. You start from Prospect Road near Goodwood to the Peggy's Cove Road at Glen Margaret (originally known as the St. Margaret's Bay Road). A second hike begins near the Keltic Lodge golf course in Cape Breton Highlands National Park. A path leads from there to a fire tower on Mount Frainey; this vantage point provides splendid views of the coastline.

Canada's most spectacular country, full of steep rock faces, mountain cirques, snow, and high forests, is in the province of Alberta. The region surrounding Banff and Lake Louise is as famous for skiers as it is for hikers and climbers. Let's examine the area in detail. Lake Louise has three main valleys—Louise, Paradise, and Moraine, with connecting trail systems. These trails provide you with a real smorgasbord of walking. Distances? Anything from one mile to ten and longer. Mirror and Agnes lakes, at altitudes of six thousand and seven thousand feet, attract many hikers. You can reach them by a trail which leaves the shore of Lake Louise just beyond the last building on the north side, to the right. A nature trail has been established between Mirror and the far end of Lake Agnes. Plants are labeled and the self-guiding leaflet gives you information on geology and animals.

Paradise Valley is another favorite Lake Louise area destination. You get there by using the main trail to Moraine Lake. Turn off to go up Paradise Creek, or, if you wish, climb the switchback trail over Saddle. The superb view and the flowers of Sheol Valley, descending the far side en route to Giant Steps and Lake Annette, are highlights. Sentinel Pass should not be attempted without walking boots. From Moraine Lake (which lies at 6,190 feet), trails head in two directions. The flatter 2½-mile hike to Consolation Lake starts in the campground area at Moraine, and ends on the lake shore with a lovely reflection view of Mt. Bident and Mt. Quadra. The trail across the outlet of Consolation Lake and along the far shore is an interesting one too.

The Banff, Alberta, region is difficult to surpass for beauty and varied hiking terrain. In fact, here you'll find just about every kind of trail, from the short stroll to the extended ramble and some well-graded trails to mountaintops (not to mention very difficult rock ascents!).

If you haven't done much hiking before, start with short trails like the one only two miles up to Tunnel Mountain, gaining only one thousand feet. Unless you make long stops you should be able to make the top in about eighty minutes, and the return trip, including time for the views at the top and a good rest, in about two hours. Where do you start this well-known ascent? Go to the Banff School of Fine Arts, and find St. Julien Avenue. The trail is marked. You'll find no water on this little mountain, so take some fruit or something to drink, especially on a warm day. Also, don't look for the tunnel—it isn't there. The railway had plans for one through the ridge but it was never built. The wonderful

IN CANADA, Banff National Park offers many vistas and some unusual names, such as the Devil's Thumb and Big Beehive, shown here. (*Canadian Govt. Travel Bureau*)

view from the summit of Tunnel Mountain makes the hike worth your time and energy. It lies like an island in the middle of a valley, which runs east and west, cutting across the ranges. Take it easy and stick to the trail, for a pleasant and rewarding walk.

If you seek an even easier hike near the town of Banff, and don't want to climb much, try the trail *around* Tunnel Mountain. Walk downstream along Bow River from the north end of Bow Bridge, to the view above Bow Falls (one mile, with the last part of the route on the road). This is a good picnic spot with a fine view of the Banff Springs Hotel and the Spray River valley framing Goat Mountain.

From here continue on the road a few yards to a sign on the right which announces "Trail to Hoodoos 2.9M." Take this trail downhill to a quiet backwater of the Bow River less than a mile away. The trail continues along the riverbank at the foot of the Tunnel Mountain cliffs to Tunnel Mountain meadows. In June and July you see a lot of mountain flowers. And there are some very large old Douglas fir trees here which survived the forest fires of a century ago because they were protected by their thick bark. The trail then climbs easily to a low east ridge of the mountain near Tunnel Mountain Campground.

Another popular excursion from Banff is a 1½-mile loop in Sundance Canyon, crossing the lively stream tumbling and splashing over the edge of Sundance Valley on its way to the Bow River. Some interesting plants grow here: purple phacelia, golden corydalis, and spotted saxifrage. The trail continues upstream for almost a mile, then climbs a little above the right bank, turns back through the woods to a fine viewpoint of Mt. Edith across the valley, and finally descends the hill to the parking lot.

Other trails near Banff include one to the Sulphur Mountain summit (three miles, or about two hours, climb 2,200 feet). The trail access is next to the gondola lift, which serves

skiers in winter. Or, beginning at the Mount Norquay parking area, you can hike up to the Amphitheatre on Cascade
Mountain (four miles one way, climb two thousand feet plus
three hundred feet on the return journey), and on to Elk
Lake (eight miles one way, with a two-thousand–foot gradual
climb). The trail from the parking area goes gently downhill
to the valley of Forty Mile Creek, a clear and lively stream
which furnishes the water for Banff Townsite. Across the
bridge the well-graded trail switchbacks up the western
slopes of Cascade Mountain to the Amphitheatre. This is a
great cleft in the side of the mountain where alpine flowers,
marmots, and pikas abide. It is also visited by goat, sheep, elk.
Partway up this trail a left fork leads toward the head of the
valley on a fairly level trail over the pass and around a ridge
of Brewster Mountain to Elk Lake, which lies in a small
hanging valley beyond, and two hundred to three hundred
feet above the pass. Here you are completely away from
Bow Valley and its familiar peaks. The lake at seven thousand feet overlooks a high and wild valley of alpine meadows
studded with alpine fir.

Farther west, British Columbia holds more adventures for
the hiker. You can get details from the Department of Recreation and Conservation, Parliament Building, Victoria,
B.C., Canada.

4 locale: hiking trails (midwest and west)

The states of Wisconsin, Michigan, and Illinois are mostly flat with occasional hillocks, and no points higher than 2,300 feet above sea level. (In Illinois the highest is 1,200 feet.) Yet people in these states—and in Indiana and Iowa—are as enthusiastic about hiking as Westerners with their fourteen-thousand-foot-high peaks. Iowa, for instance, has an excellent mountain club, the Iowa Mountaineers, who have stalked trails as far away as Africa. There is a very active Sierra Club chapter in Illinois. In Logan, Ohio, the Buckeye Trail Association takes responsibility for the Buckeye Trail, which is over 150 miles long. And Michigan's Shore to Shore Trail runs across the state from Elberta and Empire on Lake Michigan to Tawas City on Lake Huron. You'll find walks in Indiana's Dune State Park, and you can hike through almost twenty-eight thousand acres of woods in the Black Hills of South Dakota. (Your headquarters should be the Wind Cave National Park.)

Wisconsin has a bounty of foot trails that snuggle past lovely lakes, through green meadows, along brooks, and up and down the modest dales. You can plan hikes as short as a quarter of a mile or as long as thirty miles. Many trails take you to streams that offer fine fishing. Scenic and historic sights on the trails include Big Manitou Falls and Copper Falls, the superb bluffs at Devil's Lake, the historic shot tower at Tower Hill State Park, and the Indian burial mounds at Lizard Mounds State Park.

The Glacial Trail in the northern unit of the Kettle Moraine State Forest is used frequently by Boy Scouts and other organizations and is also popular for family hikes. The trail traverses many interesting geological features created by the recession of the last glacier. It is sixteen miles in length and has trailside shelters, where camping is permitted.

The Peninsula State Park, near Ephraim, Wisconsin, offers a variety of trails which are often used by vacationers. The three main trails are Sentinel Trail, Sunset Trail, and Eagle Trail. Sentinel Trail (length: two miles, about two hours) begins at Eagle Tower. It quickly enters the forest, winding through highland hardwoods, maple, beech, and oak, taking you into some of the most primitive areas of the park. The trail crosses a large open meadow which leads into a red pine forest and deer area. Walking this trail is relatively easy because there are no hills or steep climbs. The trail forms a large loop and returns to the starting place, so there is no chance to get lost.

Sunset Trail is about seven miles long and will take four to five hours to hike. You can join Sunset Trail at Welcker's Point, Weborg Point, and Tennison Bay camping areas. The Sunset Trail goes through a variety of areas. It closely follows the water's edge near Tennison Bay, crosses several open meadows, rocky bluffs, cedar forests, and two low grassy areas which are bird sanctuaries.

Eagle Trail is the most popular in the park despite its comparative steepness. Starting from Eagle Tower, you scramble over the highest bluffs in the county. The trail is about two miles long and it will take at least three hours to make the loop.

COLORADO scenery — mountains with eternal snow, cold lakes, trees and rocks — attracts many Eastern hikers to the West. (*Colorado Dept. of Public Relations*)

Of course, none of these paths reach the heights you find out West, especially in Colorado. This state has fifty-three peaks over fourteen thousand feet, most of them with well-established trails. Outside Aspen, Colorado, there is even a self-guiding nature trail for the blind. The sightless are led by a cord attached to posts past twenty-two stations with Braille descriptions of what can be smelled, touched, walked over, and heard in the area.

It would be impossible here to describe every Colorado mountain route. You can get excellent information on specific questions from the Colorado Mountain Club, 1723 East 16th Avenue, Denver, Colorado 80218. Several thousand Colorado hikers belong to this club, which has a junior division.

Much talk goes on about which Colorado trails are best. Here are some of my preferences. For an easy outing in the plains and foothills, head twenty-three miles south of Denver to Sedalia. Ask for the Rampart Range Road; once you're on it, you'll see two mighty stone pillars with the appropriate name, Devil's Head. The two-mile uphill walk won't be devilish—it shouldn't take much longer than an hour hiking below stunning granite formations, and through leafy-tree country. On top, a fire tower allows you to take a look at the instruments and at the 360-degree view. Another short and sweet trail starts 1½ miles from Lyons, Colorado (north of Boulder). Park at the rushing, pure St. Vrain Creek and head up 1,000 feet to Indian Lookout Mountain (6,534 feet). The walking distance is three miles, and even a small child can do it.

A slightly more ambitious hike in a more remote area begins near Kremmling. At the Blue Valley Resort turn sharply to the left onto the unimproved road and drive to the lower end of Cataract Lake. (Here the road branches right and a sign reads "Upper Cataract Lake 8 miles.") Follow the trail for three miles up the ridge to its junction with Gore Range Trail, marked by a sign. Follow Gore Range Trail left to Tipperary Lake. Walking distance is six miles, elevation gain 1,500 feet.

You'll also find three hundred miles of trails in the Rocky Mountain National Park, with headquarters at Estes Park, Colorado (population, 2,000; elevation 7,500 feet). The park's ranger-naturalists conduct guided hikes of various durations—two-hour, half-day, three-quarter-day, and all-day. On these field trips, they will lead you to some of the park's outstanding areas and features, such as Dream Lake, Tyndall and Andrews Glaciers, Odessa Lake, Ouzel Falls, and Lulu City, an old mining camp. While you hike, the rangers will tell you that there are more than 750 kinds of plants in the Rocky Mountain National Park. Below 9,500 feet, you encounter quaking aspen, Douglas fir, narrow-leaf cottonwood, thin-leaf alder, Rocky Mountain juniper, and blue spruce, and two species of pine (ponderosa and lodgepole) grow in profusion. During autumn, the aspen leaf turns a golden yellow and becomes very beautiful.

Above 9,500 feet, the Engelmann spruce, subalpine fir, and limber pine are the most common trees. The bog birch and plane-leaf, or "subalpine," willow are also found here.

There are literally hundreds of different kinds of wild flowers. The Colorado State flower—Colorado columbine —may be found in bloom from June through August, depending upon the elevation.

When you want to strike out on your own, the Loch Vale Trail is well trodden and well marked, and the distance (2 ½ miles both ways) should give you no trouble. (Get used to the altitude by staying at a nearby lodge for a day.) The trail begins at Glacier Gorge Junction, thirteen miles from Estes Park and a mile below Bear Lake, and leads to a glacier-watered valley which has few equals for its sheer rocky wild-

ONCE A YEAR, several hundred Colorado hikers
of all ages assemble near Boulder, then head for
the Arapahoe Glacier, half a day away. Cooks and guides
come along, too. (*Boulder Chamber of Commerce*)

ness and the glory of its wild flowers, virgin forest, and lakes. At the head of Loch Vale, Taylor Peak rises to an elevation of 13,153 feet; to the northwest is Otis Peak, almost as high; between them is Andrews Glacier; on the east is Thatchtop.

Even when the sky is gray, a hike up to Chasm Lake is exciting. You begin at the Long's Peak Campground Ranger Station. The Chasm Lake Trail is well marked. You'll find it ideal for windy days because your route tunnels through forests for two hours. Once you reach the ridge, Long's Peak is before you in all its might. One more hour and you're at the picturesque lake. Total mileage: 5½ miles up and 5½ down. You can do it in a morning, even if you take time to look for rare rocks or watch the chipmunks at play.

Colorado also has excellent and often remote hiking trails near the Maroon Bells (Aspen), in the Flattops Wilderness (Meeker), the Routt National Forest (Steamboat Springs), and in the Gore Range (Vail).

While Colorado's summer and fall weather is often clear and sunny, in Wyoming's Grand Teton National Park several hikers have died from exposure in summer. Nothing, though, matches the Grand Tetons for sheer drama.

Park service personnel can direct you to many short and long trails, all of which take you away from masses of noisy tourists who stick to their trailers in the luxurious campgrounds. Some fine trails start from Jenny Lake, which is headquarters for an excellent mountaineering school. (You can hire guides there.) One of the most spectacular trips is along the Glacier Trail. It begins at Lupine Meadows, hits a series of steep switchbacks after about a mile, and shoots up to a thundering stream in Garnet Canyon. More difficult and far longer trails (with fantastic views) lead all the way from Jenny Lake to Lake Solitude, across the Grand Teton itself (13,766 feet) down a saddle to the Middle Teton and up and across the South Teton to the park's "Moose Station."

While in Wyoming, consider also the Teton Wilderness Area (563,500 acres, 885 square miles) of back country accessible on foot. During the summer you are apt to see trumpeter swans, sandhill cranes, ducks and geese, grouse, hawks of several species, golden and bald eagles, coyote, ground squirrels, black bears, ravens . . . possibly even beaver, marten, bobcat, otter, or mink.

Thousands of elk are scattered through the forest. Occasionally, you will find bighorn sheep in early morning and late evening, particularly along the Gros Ventre River around Red Hills, along the lower end of Crystal Creek.

The Teton Wilderness Area offers views of timber, waterfalls, wide meadows, lakes and streams (with excellent fishing), and broad valleys. Along the continental divide, you see steep canyons and barren alpine country where snowfall is not uncommon in July.

Wyoming's Yellowstone Park is also ideal hiking country. Want to get away from it all? Try the Wind River Range for solitude. Montana's Glacier National Park is a vast region for hikers, and you can find many worthwhile destinations in Montana and Idaho's Selway-Bitterroot Wilderness. In Utah, you can find all kinds of trail up and down the Wasatch Range, near Salt Lake City. And there are fine, easy nature trails in the Dinosaur National Monument.

California has well-developed trail systems. In the Yosemite National Park, for example, there are 761,000 acres, and a trail network that forbids bicycles, motorbikes, and cars. Among the better-known foot trips are the Half Dome Trail (sixteen miles round trip, or about twelve hours!), the even longer (seventeen miles, also twelve hours) Panorama Trail, and the Vernal-Nevada Falls Trail, which is fine for novices (only six miles round trip, about six hours). The latter path starts at the Happy Isles Bridge; it's less than a mile to view Vernal Falls. During the early spring and summer this trail is

THERE ARE MANY possibilities for backpackers
in the high state of Montana. (*U.S. Forest Service*)

SOME OF THE MOST remote and lovely hiking
country can be found in Idaho. The state gets
fewer tourists than Colorado, and you can
discover many peaceful nooks in the
Sawtooth Mountain range. (*Idaho Dept. of Commerce*)

wet and sometimes slippery. From the top of Vernal Falls it's another two miles to the top of Nevada Fall via a series of fairly steep switchbacks. Guardrails are there for your safety.

The Panorama Trail begins at Glacier Point, and then descends 1½ miles (1,300 feet) to pass across the top of Illilouette Fall, after which you climb up and around the shoulder above Panorama Cliffs. You then descend by either the horse trail or foot trail. A popular, though very strenuous, all-day hike is to go up the Glacier Point Four Mile Trail and return to the Valley via the Panorama Trail. Take water!

Half Dome Trail starts at Happy Isles in Yosemite. Follow the Vernal–Nevada Falls Trail to the top of Nevada Fall and on into the Little Yosemite Valley. The trail then branches off to the left along the Clouds Rest Trail around the back side of Half Dome for 1½ miles where it again branches to the left for 2 miles to the base of Half Dome. The last six hundred feet are very steep and can be climbed only with the aid of cables. You may prefer to make the hike in two days and camp in the Little Yosemite Valley. Again, take water.

In California, you can also hike in the Kings Canyon National Park, in the Lassen Volcanic National Park, and in the Sequoia National Park. If you've tried them all and dream of a really long backpacking trip, think of the John Muir Trail. It goes on for 218 miles, tracing the backbone of the Sierra Nevada Range between Yosemite Valley on the north and Whitney Portal on the south. Over this entire route the trail makes contact with roads in only four places: Yosemite Valley, Tuolumne Meadows, Devils Postpile National Monument, and Whitney Portal. Thirty-six miles of the trail lie within the boundaries of Yosemite National Park. The remainder lies in the Sierra, Inyo, and Mono national

THE SUMMIT OF California's Mount Whitney is still thirteen miles away from these hikers. Is the forest ranger telling the boys that they're not well enough dressed for the long venture? (*U.S. Forest Service*)

forests and in Sequoia and Kings Canyon national parks.

The best time to travel the trail is between July 15 and September 15, depending upon snow conditions. Remember that most of the trail is at elevations of more than seven thousand feet, and in some places it goes above thirteen thousand feet. Fire permits are required and you can't take firearms.

If you have many weeks at your disposal (and good legs plus reliable, sturdy companions), consider the Pacific Crest Trail. It extends from Washington all the way to Mexico. It runs down the backbone of the Cascade Mountains in Washington and Oregon, through the Sierra Nevada Mountains in California, to a final 406 miles of desert. It is mainly a foot trail, but packhorses and burros are also used. In the Cascades (where you also find Mount Rainier and other high peaks) you'll be treated to a generous share of America's most verdant forests, tallest and oldest trees, high mountains, and most breathtaking waterfalls. The golden trout and the almost extinct giant condor are found here and the mountains abound with deer, black bear, and other interesting varieties of game.

The Pacific Crest Trail is continuously passable for 2,313 miles, from border to border. The segments in California are known as the Lava Crest Trail, the Sierra Trail, and the Desert Crest Trail. Through Oregon's Cascades, the trail is the Oregon Skyline Trail. The portion in Washington is known as the Cascade Crest Trail.

In Washington, the Pacific Crest Trail moves south along the high ridges of the Cascade Mountains, threading through many famous mountain passes and the Okanogan, Mount Baker, Wenatchee, Snoqualmie, and Gifford Pinchot national forests. The most spectacular scenery is found in the North Cascade Primitive Area, Glacier Peak Wilderness, Mount Rainier National Park, Goat Rocks Wilderness, and

Mount Adams Wilderness. From the high, barren ridges there are many outstanding views of mountain ranges, snow-covered peaks, and glaciers. Alpine meadows with clear springs and brooks, small lakes, and rushing rivers are frequently found. Mountain goat, elk, deer, bear, rock rabbit, marmot, grouse, and ptarmigan add interest. At lower altitudes, dense stands of Douglas fir predominate on the western slopes. Abandoned mines, old frontier towns, and other relics of pioneer days still remain for you to see.

At the Columbia River, the Pacific Crest Trail crosses from Washington to Oregon on the Bridge of the Gods. In Oregon, as in Washington, the trail follows the ridges of the Cascades much of the distance and stays largely on federal lands. The trail crosses the Mount Hood, Willamette, Deschutes, Umpqua, Rogue River, and Winema National Forests. Glacial moraines and ice fields are visible at Mount Hood where the trail passes the Timberline Lodge and ski area. Farther south, the trail leads through the Mount Jefferson Primitive Area, the Mount Washington Wilderness with its lava flows and basalt columns, the striking Three Sisters Wilderness, and the Diamond Peak Wilderness. A section of the trail crosses Crater Lake National Park, passing the uniquely beautiful lake. En route are the Pumice Desert, lodgepole and yellow pine forests, and waters with superb trout fishing.

The California portion of the trail generally follows the highest ridges of the Sierra Nevada. Fourteen national forests are crossed, beginning with the Klamath National Forest on the California-Oregon state line. An almost endless number of exhilarating experiences await you as you hike through the Marble Mountain Wilderness, Thousand Lakes Wilderness, Donner Pass, Minarets Wilderness, Devils Postpile National Monument, Kings Canyon National Park, Sequoia National Park, and Devils Canyon–Bear Canyon Primitive Area. The trail passes through several state parks, crosses the San Andreas Fault, and after leaving the Cleveland National Forest finally terminates at the Mexican border some forty miles southeast of San Diego.

Don't forget that there are many trails in the Southwest.

New Mexico, which calls itself the "Land of Enchantment," ranges in altitude from 2,850 feet to 13,151 feet above sea level, and has twenty million acres of wooded land. (The U.S. Forest Service administers more than 8½ million acres here.)

Two branches of a famed nineteenth-century trading route that extended to the provincial capital of Santa Fe— then part of Mexico—passed through northeastern New Mexico. Ruts of the trail are still visible near the ruins of Fort Union. This area has great variety. There are the towering Sangre de Cristo Mountains and the giant Pecos Wilderness Area, over 100,000 acres of untouched forest. Near Bandera Crater is a series of perpetual ice caves, and to the south, the Gila National Forest includes a sprawling wilderness area where motor vehicles are forbidden but hikers are always welcome.

For more information, write to the National Park Service, Washington, D.C. 20240, or to the U.S. Forest Service, Washington, D.C. 20250.

Perhaps you live—or visit—even farther north, in Alaska. Here you can hike on some 283,000,000 acres of public lands, much of it high. There are good trails near the major Alaskan cities. North of Fairbanks, for example, you'll find the popular White Mountains Trail. And twelve miles south of Anchorage, you can clamber up to McHugh Peak, for a lovely view. Ambitious and able backpackers will have their hearts set on the "Old Chilkoot Trail." To get from beginning to end you'll need four days. For more details, you can write to the Mountaineering Club of Alaska, P.O. Box 2037, Anchorage, Alaska 99501.

And remember to bring warm clothes!

5 motivations:
why do they climb?

There are as many reasons for climbing mountains as there are people. For some, mountaineering is exploration. You become an adventurer. You never know what is around the next corner. Scale the sheer cliffs of the Hudson River valley in New York State, and all at once you'll be face to face with two young owls. When climbers poked up the enormous reddish rocks of the Mesa Verde National Park, they gasped. Here were cliff dwellings of a civilization going back to the year 1000. Teton guides have stepped on ancient Indian arrows, on Indian necklaces and trinkets. In Idaho, you may come upon the nest of a hawk, or suddenly look into the eyes of mountain sheep. Elsewhere, in high meadows, you will encounter deer or antelope. When a party of young climbers went to sleep near a forlorn mountain creek in Wyoming, they awoke to find themselves surrounded by a dozen (harmless) porcupines.

Adventure? You move up and up, and the higher you go, the more mysterious it becomes. You are reaching high peaks in the wilderness that make you think you are on another planet. And some of the delight of still edging higher may stem from the feeling that you're perhaps the first person up here. Deep within you, there is a suspicion that you have no right to be in this high region, that you're an interloper, that you're in another world. This is one reason why climbers like to be the first on a peak. And the sense of exploration drives climbers to mountains farther and farther away: first to their backyard hills, then to the Rockies, the Alps, and finally the Andes in South America, or Kilimanjaro in Africa.

Mountain climbing is a wonderful excuse for voyages. No year goes by when some mountain-club members don't strike out for Peru or Alaska or Europe. And a few—very few—climbers journey to the Himalayas, the "Roof of the World," perhaps to search for the Abominable Snowman. In his desire for adventure, the mountain explorer is like the archaeologist, who digs into the earth to find houses and treasures of ancient civilizations. And like the men who dive for old coins or cross the Atlantic in a rickety sailboat. Some climbers feel as motivated by this search as the astronauts who will eventually rocket to Mars.

Naturally, some men have been attracted to climbing because they want to find out more about the physical nature of mountains and about human reactions. Mountain climbers include glaciologists, geologists, weather experts, physicists, physicians, prospectors, all interested in the mountains. As far back as 1787, Horace de Saussure, a Swiss, scaled Mont Blanc mainly for the sake of science. What was the air like at fifteen thousand feet? What sort of temperatures would he find? What did crevasses conceal? Even John Muir, the sensitive American hiker, climber, and beauty worshiper, sought more in the Sierra Nevadas than just grandeur. "Have been exploring the glaciers that lie on the head waters of San Joaquin, and Owen's Rivers, measuring and studying their movements, trends, moraines," Muir wrote proudly in one of his journals. The first American Everest expedition included a geographer, a sociologist, and three medical doctors who

JAMES WHITTAKER on Everest. (*Recreational Equipment, Inc.*)

wanted to know more about the terrific altitude, and what it did to men. They checked on respiration and heartbeats, on behavior under stress; they measured solar radiation, and shipped pieces of a glacier to Stateside labs for examination. The expedition leader once called them "my climbing egg-heads." But they were really just a few of the thousands of men who have done, and do, their research in the mountains.

You do not have to climb Everest yourself to learn more about the world above you. Every weekend, men and boys set out for the Catskills, the White Mountains, the Green Mountains, the Rockies in New Mexico, or the Cascades. They may carry a magnifying glass and a geologist's rock hammer. Rocks are fascinating subjects to study, and a good-enough reason to climb. You will find hundreds of rock varieties and mixtures. If you look long enough, you may also find fossils—leaves that have become stone and are now embedded in rock, shells that may be thousands of years old, or the bones of extinct animals. You may find lava of dead volcanoes or ancient petrified ferns. For the geologist, rock is the be-all and end-all; he can tell a hundred things. But even for the rest of us, the glitter of a silver vein in granite is enough.

Why do they climb?

The real mountaineer seeks the unknown; he wants to go beyond the rim of experience. The travel entails danger, and the experienced climber knows that. Danger is sweet to him; he doesn't fear it.

Not long ago, a bronzed lean youth from Seattle, Washington, turned up at Camp Muir on Mount Rainier. He had never climbed before, but he was trying it. His reason? "I've flown a plane. I've dived under the sea. I've raced a car. Now I want to climb." Fortunately he had come with a group of friends who knew Rainier well.

It is a mighty mountain, and although you're with others,

you relish the silence and the solitude. There is danger, but it gives you more strength, more alertness. You move cautiously, roped onto two companions. The ice must be probed for hidden crevasses and for unsafe snowbridges. Your leader watches out for every crack. He listens to every sound. Sometimes you come to an icy fissure. You must jump across. Can you do it? You can, and your ax is held ready in your hands. If you slip, the sharp metal point must sink into the glacier like an anchor into the sea. Sometimes you walk alongside the void, which may be a hundred feet deep. Crevasses have strange hues of blue and green, and the peril of falling in makes your spine tingle. When you descend to the valley again, you feel good inside. You are warm with pride. At about eight thousand feet, you're out of the ice, and on the trails. You see a few people in tennis shoes. They'll never go where you've been, you think to yourself. Then, at 5,400 feet, you're at the Paradise Inn, complete with its soda fountain and postcard stands. You're amused. There are a lot of visitors in their Sunday best, with shoes well shined. They're getting out of automobiles to view the summit of Mt. Rainier through coin-operated telescopes.

The late Wilfrid Noyce, the British Alpinist and writer, once pointed out the difference between tourists and climbers. The climber has to flee back to something primitive. He wants to get away from civilization. He may earn his living in a hospital or factory or office. But from time to time, as Noyce puts it, "the climber has the irresistible urge to tear off his stiff collar and tie, don old clothes, sweat and shiver, dig his fingers into the wet earth, and sleep on the hard ground." He wants to get back to the days of the pioneer, the Western mountain man or the Swiss chamois hunter. Unlike the skier, who is very fashion-conscious these days, the climber can wear anything; he must merely be protected from the elements. Some ski areas now resemble cities; long lines snake at the tows; the parking lots and cafeterias can be crowded, and the runs resemble turnpikes. The climber wants to escape from these human masses. And he wants to get out of the city.

There is a junior editor in New York who works in a cubicle of an office without windows. When he goes out for lunch, he sees the walls of a restaurant, and the gray pavement and the dirty streets. He lives in an apartment where he glimpses only brick walls through the window. No sky, no greenery. But he makes up for it on Sunday when he hikes and climbs. A boy I know works in a Salt Lake City photo lab. He is in the darkness from Monday to Friday. And he waits hungrily for the weekend when he can flee up to the crags and towers and hanging meadows of the Wasatch Range, which is as beautiful as the Italian Alps. He is in the light up there. And he is free. Not in vain did the "Mountaineers of Seattle" title a book *The Freedom of the Hills*. There are no streets in the high peaks. No packed subways. No cars. No crowded department stores. No noisy machines. You have left algebra or unpleasant people or a dull job in the valley. You can look down on conformity and on laws and conventions. You get no telegrams. You see no banks, and so forget financial worries. You can peel off school problems, and strip the pressures of commerce. You're free.

And you're in a world of beauty that dazzles, amazes, startles, soothes you. In fact, many people take to climbing just for the vistas. John Ruskin, the English writer, once said that mountains to him were the beginning and the end of all natural scenery, that nothing else existed. Eric Shipton, the famed English climber, is seized with "an exaltation of feeling" every time he climbs. John Muir wrote a half-dozen books just about the lakes and ice fields and trees of the Sierras. Poets like Shelley, Byron, and Wordsworth sing out at the sight of even small elevations. James Ramsey Ullman

SOME OF THE most dazzling and stunning mountain landscapes are found among the glaciers and snows of the Cascades. This picture was taken on one of the easier peaks, Mount Hood. No climber would go unroped into such regions. (*Timberline Lodge*)

has written his most inspired novels and books amid the scenery of Switzerland and Nepal. Composers have put symphonies to paper under the peaks, and some painters choose no other subject for their canvases. The mountain spell can be just as strong for the rest of us, old or young.

A boy who spent a night on Long's Peak in Colorado later said he gasped at the sight of the stars. "They were as shiny as lanterns," he said. "My head seemed to be in the Milky Way." On clear mornings in the high regions, there is the ritual of the sun; it touches the topmost peak with orange-red color, which slowly flows downward like wet paint. The valley is still dark, then turns blue, with wisps of mist, until the sun creeps down there, too, illuminating the pinheads that are houses and the white threads of roads. There are constant changes and surprises. If you stand on Mount Hood, you may have a cottony sea of clouds billowing below you, shutting out the rest of Oregon. Approach the Tetons in Wyoming for the first time. One moment it may be snowing or raining; the next, the formidable range of stone blazes in the sunlight. Spend the day in the Tetons, and you'll marvel at the rich colors of the rocks and pastures and forests in the evening. It is true that not *all* people see this beauty, or are overwhelmed by it. For some climbers it is unimportant; but for most, the senses are stirred to a high pitch. This is perhaps why so many climbers bring cameras. They want to hold on to the picture for life, on film.

Why do men climb mountains? Some, simply for the exercise. Gaston Rebuffat, the famed French guide, once said: "To me climbing is meditation and physical action." For many people, physical action alone suffices. There is a great satisfaction in using your body for motion and not for sitting in the bleachers at some spectator sport, sucking popsicles. In the mountains you're giving every muscle and organ a chance. You discover the capabilities of the human body. With the proper training, you can often go up a trail for hours without fatigue. And every moment you climb, you know that the toil of limbs is good for you. The blood pulses through your veins and warms your skin; oxygen reaches your tissues. Unlike in the city, your innards are functioning beautifully on the mountain. You're aware of the power of your lungs, of your strong heartbeat. But there is still more.

You may simply long to learn a new skill. Rock climbing will give you many things to learn. For instance, it takes practice to hammer a piton into rock until it sticks solidly. One day you find just the right crack and the right angle. Your hammer hits, and you hear the romantic rising sound of steel on steel. You become competent in the use of hardware. This is very satisfying to many climbers. From easy rocks, you graduate to difficult ones, and one summer, you manage to scale a four-hundred-foot stone wall as straight up as a skyscraper. Even professional guides feel pride after forty years of climbing to do an impossible face, a slick, no-hand-hold face. Of course, the summit itself is all that counts for many people. They went all the way! They made it! They reached the peak. This is the climax which has moved experienced climbers to tears. "I was born all over again!" said Rebuffat of his first summit ascent as a boy. "I felt nothing but rapture!" said Maurice Herzog about the chilly summit of Annapurna. Anyway, your country's flag is up there, or your name is in the summit book. It's all yours. You got to the top!

Is it really so important to make a peak or bust? Not all climbers think so. James Ramsey Ullman observed that "the spirit of pure mountaineering" can be enough. You don't always have to get to the top. The game can be more important than the summit.

A few climbers want to set odd records. An English pro-

THE CONQUEST of a summit is unforgettable. (*R. Toepher*)

fessor at North Carolina State University, for example, has climbed Pikes Peak 308 times. He climbs this Colorado peak every Fourth of July. He doesn't do it once. No, he's only happy after he has three climbs in one day under his belt. This sort of oddity has been carried to an extreme by a Texan, Bill Williams. He pushed a peanut to the peak of Pikes Peak. It took him twenty days, during which he wore out eighty-five pairs of pants.

Still other climbers are just interested in collecting summits that are over a certain height. A fellow from Denver, Colorado, is a good example of this. Views don't interest him. But he has climbed all fifty-four Colorado peaks over fourteen thousand feet. He says, "I'm not interested in thirteen-thousanders. I have a vendetta against the fourteeners. If I don't make it the first time, I try again. I was turned back four times by bad weather from Mount Holy Cross. The fifth time, I was in luck and made it. I collect these peaks like antlers."

This man climbs alone, which is not recommended. He misses the best part of climbing: other human beings who also want to accomplish something. In the mountains, cut off from the rest of the world, the focus is on people, and people are much more interesting. If they are lucky, they become a team. In a far-flung tent, they share everything. They know they are responsible for each other's life. Even selfish persons, once they are pitted with others against a mountain, suddenly become considerate. Sometimes, when they part, they may never see each other again. But often, climbing creates a bond. The rope has linked them. They become friends for life. This is perhaps the most worthwhile reason for climbing. As Woodrow Wilson Sayre, a well-known American climber, once put it more eloquently, "Real friendship is increasingly difficult. We hurry so much, we move, we change jobs, we juggle a hundred responsibilities.

GETTING TO KNOW other members of your team
is one of the most important rewards
of mountaineering. (*Colorado Outdoor Sports Corp.*)

How often do we see our best friends? Once a week? Once a
month? Less than that? If we hardly see them, can we really
share joy and tragedy with them? I think men are made for a
deeper sort of friendship. If they miss it, they miss something
very important in life. Men are made for the close warmth
tested in the danger and adversity of mountains."

6 traits:
what makes
a good climber?

The qualities of a good climber have as much to do with character as with physique. You need emotional strength as well as physical. This means determination, courage (but not overconfidence), coolness, team spirit. You can't always show your feelings if you're weary or chilled. Whenever a novice climber complains to one mountain guide that he's cold or tired, the guide's face breaks into a smile. "You know," he will say gently, "someone here is probably colder than you. And even more tired." On difficult climbs, this control of emotions is especially important.

You can't be high-strung or get hysterical when the chips are down. One of the most experienced German climbers, Toni Hiebeler, was on the Eiger North wall in Switzerland when he consulted his barometer one evening. To his horror, it had dropped four points in a few hours. This was an almost sure sign of a storm. But Hiebeler kept quiet about his findings, just as a doctor sometimes withholds bad news from a patient when nothing can be improved by his knowing. Hiebeler had enough self-control not to upset his comrades. They waited out the night; in the morning, the weather turned out to be bright, and they reached the top.

The best climbers try not to make too much fuss when

WELL-KNOWN CLIMBERS such as Toni Hiebeler have achieved difficult mountaineering feats by keeping cool. Hiebeler's steady nerves helped his team climb Switzerland's most difficult peak, the Eiger North Face. (*Rudolf Rohr*)

they're sick. Some years back, an American named Art Ginkley was stricken with thrombophlebitis—a high-altitude blood clot—at twenty-five thousand feet. He got medical attention, but when his friends asked him how he was, he'd try a smile and say, "Just fine." At times, thirst can be racking you so much that—like the shipwrecked man—you find the smallest drop of moisture a blessing. Yet you'd make a climb more difficult for your teammates by complaining. Even on a small rock wall you're badly off if there is someone along who goes to pieces too easily. Or who wants too much personal glory. In short, a good mountaineer is selfless. He must be able to get along with all types of people.

This is recognized in the motto of the famous Outward Bound Camps, where boys are trained to face physical hardships. The motto goes like this: "To think of others before ourselves, and to realize the need for helping without thought of reward, and with this kindness a cheerfulness that becomes infectious and helps others in times of stress and strain."

There is no *sure* way to ensure that a harmonious group in the valley will remain harmonious on the mountain. Differences in personality and physical ability are brought out rapidly after you leave for the heights. Once these differences begin to arise, you must adjust yourself.

Mountaineering actually strips character down to the bones. A few minutes on a rock spire with a person can tell you more about him than five joint trips to Disneyland. On a ledge, no one can fake anything. It is often said that "two days on a mountain will show you more about a person than knowing him in the valley for twenty years." The ideal situation was illustrated in the Everest climb. When Jim Whittaker and the Sherpa with him had almost reached this highest point of our planet and were a few steps from their 29,028-foot aim, Whittaker said, "You go first." "No, you!"

GROUP HARMONY is the job for every individual.
A hike or climb can be ruined
by the irresponsibility of one person.
(*U.S. Forest Service*)

said the Sherpa. "Go ahead." "No, you." Then, at last, James Whittaker claimed his prize, the summit of Mt. Everest. It's unlikely that you'll go to the Himalayas or join an expedition and make a name for yourself. Yet you can learn a great deal from the character makeup of famous mountaineers. If you imitate their example, you'll be on the right track even on the small boulder outside your home town. What are the celebrated climbers really like?

Great climbers are usually unassuming people. They don't become arrogant about their achievements. Take Gaston Rebuffat, for instance. He has done every difficult peak in the Alps, and several in the Himalayas, yet you can't tell it when you see him. One of the great European climbers, Gino Solda, is a simple man. Layton Kor—one of the best Americans—is all humility. These traits apply to all great climbers. They have been too often and too long in the immensity of the mountain landscape to feel like giants. They know they are dwarfed by the much bigger rocks, by the bulky Tetons that rise straight up from a valley floor, or by an enormous ice hunk like Rainier.

People feel justly proud after they have struggled up to a summit; in fact, it is natural to brag a little. "Imagine!" you tell your parents or a friend. "I climbed Mt. Olympus!" But it is also true that some young climbers become arrogant about their achievements. This is bad. If you happen to be the most skilled of three boys and thus are in charge on a rock scramble, it is especially important to think of the rest of your group.

Let the praise come from others. You must remember that success is not due solely to you and your effort, but to the combined effort, interest, and ability of the group, and so you share your success with them. The leader must develop a great respect for the dignity and rights of everyone, and understand that everybody should have an opportunity to show what he can do.

Strangely enough, there is a "climbing grapevine." Word about climbing show-offs gets around. One daredevil, for instance, goofed so often in the mountains that everyone knew about this man. He had three bad crackups, yet he still did foolish things. According to an acquaintance, "a hush would fall in his climbing club whenever he showed his face. No one wanted to climb with him."

You need courage, naturally. Courage can be acquired with experience and is the result of good leadership. Courage ought to be tempered with prudence, however. You must keep thinking, "Will this rock be safe? Am I using the best rock crack to go up? Will my rope dislodge a boulder that falls on someone below? Am I moving too fast?" You need to know your climbing ABC's. This takes time.

Remember that rock climbing isn't for everyone. If you've tried it a few times and don't like it, choose another sport, or continue hiking. Some people can never get used to heights and quickly drop out. Others find the mental strain of searching for correct handholds and footholds almost unbearable. Still others won't put up with the exertion. Even a well-known Western football coach gave up climbing after one attempt. "This was my first time and my last," he said. "And I have two pieces of advice for climbers. In the first place, don't go. In the second place, if you must go, ride a horse!"

The best climbers have an interest in science. Can you, for instance, tell the humidity from a sunset? Figure the distance of a thunderstorm from your mountain location? Tell from the shape of a snowy slope when (and why) an avalanche might come down? Calculate how much longer it takes to cook an egg at ten thousand feet than at sea level? Find your position on a map? Read a compass accurately? Know your position from the stars? Do you *like* to solve technical problems?

Topnotch climbers are usually good with their hands.

IT TAKES GREAT courage to jump across crevasses, but prudence is equally important. This mountaineer didn't bother with a rope—a foolish act that could cost his life. (*Swiss National Tourist Office*)

When Paul Petzoldt—who started the Teton National Park Mountaineering School—was a boy, he found himself stuck on a perpendicular glacier slope. He had no ice ax or crampons, and he was alone. He probed his pockets and discovered that he'd brought a pocket knife. He snapped it open and painstakingly cut footholds and handholds out of the ice. This saved his life.

The sense for the practical will crop up again and again if you go to the mountains. You'll have to put up a tent, which consists of so many stakes, pegs, guy lines, and other pieces. You must learn to make three different climbing rope knots that require as many as six motions each. You must be able to choose the right steel spike (called a piton) from ten such pitons for a certain rock crack, rig up a splint for someone's fractured hand, put on a pair of steel crampons for a glacier ascent so well that they *stay* on all day. You may be called upon to do all these things and others.

The best climbers have strong shoulders and hands, well-trained legs and arms. Fitness is important even on rock scrambles that take only a morning. You step upward; you coordinate legs and arms; you use your fingers and palms; you push yourself through a chimney by the strength of your back and feet; you lean out from a rock like a sailor, you arch your back. Legs straddled against the slabs, you walk backward and downward by means of a rope.

So you must be in sound physical shape. One climbing organization suggests that all its members do the following:

- Do at least ten push-ups each morning and night.
- Do at least five chin-ups each morning and night.
- Run a mile every day.
- Walk or run to and from school or work instead of driving.
- Climb stairs. Avoid the elevator.
- Give up tobacco and alcohol.

Fitness is more important than brute strength. You can make up for the lack of muscle power with agility, coordination, balance. For this reason, even a frail girl can learn to climb. The so-called weaker sex can often build up strong stamina. One summer, for example, the Colorado Mountain Club made an ascent of a fourteen-thousand-foot-high peak. There were some fifty climbers, including some inexperienced young men. After three hours, two women were scrambling ahead. There were five gals who strode up to the summit before most of the men. The ladies were already on the return trip when one boy in his twenties just staggered to the saddle of the mountain.

Climbing is more difficult for overweight persons unless they're in exceptional condition, which is rare. Too much girth can also cause difficulties in the rocks.

Lean or fat, you'll often call on reserves you never thought possible. A boy who has gone through an Outward Bound Training Camp puts it this way: "Frequently boys bitterly regret having volunteered for some mountain expedition, but necessity is the mother of invention; they cope somehow, and come out of it bigger and better versions of themselves. I am convinced that everyone has a wealth of potentialities which are never tapped. A man might imagine all his life that he cannot jump a five-bar gate, until chased by a bull."

The history of mountaineering is full of feats of endurance. It took five hours to put up a ledge tent on an Alaskan expedition, for instance. The climbers were all in their late teens; to make the summit, they forged ahead for twenty-five hours without sleep. Or take the conquest of Annapurna. Here, Maurice Herzog, Lionel Terray, and their friends showed superhuman stamina. After reaching the summit, they got into a blizzard. It blew so hard at night that they couldn't sleep because they had to hold onto their tent poles.

IT IS NOT UNUSUAL for women to match a man's hiking stamina. This old photo shows Swiss ladies starting out on a hike. (*Swiss National Tourist Office*)

They spent another night in a crevasse and were all but buried by an avalanche. They got lost on the way down, and walked miles with frozen hands and frozen feet. Yet they survived.

Naturally, your own battles with the mountains won't require such do-or-die extremes. In the end, the most important trait is still the sheer love for the outdoors. This means braving a frequent change of weather. Many times in the afternoon, a few clouds come out of nowhere. You're already close to the summit. Soon a little rain runs down your cheeks, and you don't mind. Ten minutes later, a few hundred feet higher, your parka hood goes up. Hail is drumming a concerto on the cloth. Then you're on top! Sunshine! And you can survey the trek and the morning's work, warm pride in your chest. In the afternoon, when it's all over, and you're in the valley, you once more turn your head. You've been up there! *You!*

7 techniques:
the abc of rock climbing

The best way to learn the fine points of rock climbing is to take one of the country's many courses given by special mountaineering schools. The next best way is to join one of the frequent spring and summer classes organized by mountaineering clubs. Another possibility is to go climbing with an experienced friend and watch him in action. Study his motions and copy them. Even for a simple, easy climb—and especially for a more difficult one—motions are never sudden, jerky, brusque. They're smooth. You'll notice this when you see a motion picture of a top climber in action. Study the movements of Gaston Rebuffat, for instance. You'll notice that he ascends the steepest wall with a catlike grace. It is as if it were not a perpendicular wall at all, but a staircase. He doesn't jump. He never lunges. He never hurries.

Wherever you learn, you begin with "balance climbing." This simply means that you utilize no ropes or hardware. You're straight over your feet. There are many rock slabs and a succession of steps where such upright walking—up or down—should give you no trouble. Beginners sometimes start crawling, but this is not necessary. Walking up a ramp-like rock is the least tiring way to move, since the weight is

You must lean *away* from the rock to be safe. (*German Press Ministry*)

carried mainly by your feet, freeing your hands for slight handholds when these are needed for balance.

With the right kind of rubber—or Vibram—soles you can step up very steep slopes relying on friction alone. Balance your body over your feet and *don't lean in*, because this lessens the weight on your soles and so reduces the friction. Repeat: Don't lean in! Rhythm is necessary for balance climbing, too. Just keep going slowly, steadily. "You should 'flow' over the rock," says an instructor of the Sierra Club in San Diego, California. "No stop-and-go movements! It's no different from the normal type of walking you do every day except that it is adapted to steep and irregular terrain."

After some balance climbing, you will graduate to steeper rocks where you begin to use not only your feet but your hands as well. Remember that on steeper rocks you require a "three-point support" at all times. This is an old, established principle among climbers. It simply means that three points of your body—two hands and one foot, for instance, or one hand and both feet—must be in contact with the rock. The remaining hand or foot is free to reach for the next hold or step.

A foothold can be a ledge or a rock shelf or a rock crack. You can move upward with the help of these footholds and handholds. Progress is still made by a shifting of balance. In placing your foot on such a hold, use the edge of your foot rather than the toes. The type of boot you are wearing will determine how narrow and inclined a ledge may be and still provide a safe hold. Stiff rubber with a narrow welt will provide the best stance on narrow footholds.

Do not use your knee on a hold. It is uncomfortable to put weight on a knee. Handholds, sometimes only fingerholds, are often used for balance while one foot reaches higher, but they can also help to lift the weight of the body.

Remember that if you climb among loose rocks you must

IT IS IMPORTANT that you keep your feet
well wedged into a rock crack while you test the
next handhold. Only then can you trust your
full body weight to it. (*Colorado Outward Bound School*)

move in such a way that no stones fall on any members of your group. In loose-rock gullies a group has to "bunch" very close together. If a stone should get dislodged under your feet or hands and begins to tumble, you should call a warning, *"Rock!"* You must also be careful about your holds. On occasion, rock is rotten, and something that looks like a beautiful handhold may crumble if you put your weight on it. You should notice the quality of the rock and carefully test any hold before trusting your full weight to it. Experienced climbers never grip tree branches.

After the cliffs get steeper and the holds smaller your instructor will probably begin to use a rope. For many climbers, this is an exciting moment. Why the rope? The rope is just a safety measure—you do not climb up the rope, or hold onto it for balance, and it is not used to *pull* you up over difficult spots. You're not being hauled up. Your climbing is still done by means of holds on the rock itself. The rope is simply there to catch you if you fall, and you should climb as if it were not there at all. For your protection, make sure it goes between you and your companion in as straight a line as possible. Keeping it between your hands will usually take care of this.

It is important that you climb carefully and are secure at all times. It is a poor and dangerous practice to jump for handholds. If you can't get at a hold you want, you do not use that hold. Use a different one. You'll also notice that your leader avoids chinning up whenever he can. Your hands and arms are mostly for balance. You don't hang from a rock as if it were a chinning bar. Instead, the feet do most of the hard climbing labor.

How about climbing *down?* You may find it a little more difficult, especially at first. You're more tired and you're also more likely to look straight down and see the bottom. You get the feeling that you're more exposed and in a more delicate position. With good leadership or instruction, you'll quickly get over these fears, especially if you're in your teens.

Confidence will come from making a descent safely. (In any case you're on a rope and are not likely to hurt yourself if you do slip.) You descend all but the steepest and most difficult grades by facing toward the valley, and *not* toward the rock. (Your back should be toward the rock.) Sometimes when the terrain is not too steep, you can use pressure holds on your way down. Your hands and arms act as a counterforce. By sitting down and facing outward you place your center of gravity close to the rock. Without using the seat of your trousers you will find that you can ease yourself down by means of a succession of pressure holds, both hand and feet. A good hold can be used first by one foot and then by a hand. Facing sideways is next best and facing in is least desirable, as your view is almost nil. However, very steep faces with good holds should only be climbed down facing in.

The counterforce principle can also be applied on your way up. If you face a long vertical crack, for instance, you can put both hands in and pull outward. This counterforce will give you a good hold while you move higher. You can use the same principle in going up a "chimney." A chimney consists of two vertical or nearly vertical walls, facing each other, one to three feet apart, and generally devoid of holds. The width of the chimney determines the method of climbing used. One method is to place the back against one wall and the feet against the opposite side, somewhat lower than the back. Your hands are used to provide alternating cross pressure. One foot is moved up, then the back, then the other foot. The holding force is the friction created by back and feet being pressed against opposite walls.

If one wall is smoother than the other, keep one foot under

COUNTERFORCE brought the climber up the tightly set rocks on the left and onto the boulder. Note the hard hat. This helmet is good insurance against falling rocks. (*Steve Miller*)

THIS IS A CHIMNEY. It is climbed by means of the counterforce system. You push with hands and feet against the rock, edging upward. If the chimney is very tight, you'll also have to use your shoulders. Each motion will bring you a little higher. (*Austrian Tourist Office*)

the body against the smoother side and the other foot on the opposite side. This way a continuous counterforce is applied.

When the crack narrows down and cannot be entered and is not exactly vertical, a method called "the lie back" is used. Both hands grip one edge of the crack and pull against the feet which are pressing at right angles on the opposite edge of the crack. It is usually easier if hands and feet are not close together. But don't try the "lie-back" until an experienced climber has demonstrated it to you.

Belaying

Belaying is the climbing term for use of the rope as a means of security. There are several kinds of belays; the easiest is the "static belay." Here you're held from above by a well-anchored, well-entrenched belayer. This belayer, if he is experienced, will take the danger out of a fall. If you should lose your grip and tumble down, the capable belayer will be able to hold you. In "static climbing," which is the least complicated kind of climbing, your static belayer is always ahead of you. He is the leader and usually the best climber in the group. He decides which way to go and he is responsible for your safety. On the way down, the belayer is last, so that he can once more hold you. When you go to mountaineering school, you'll be taught belaying because it's so important and all climbers should know how the system works. "Belaying is half of rock climbing," says Henry Mandolf, Sierra Club instructor, adding, "The success of the climb depends on the belayer. He must be trustworthy. He must be aware of his responsibility."

What exactly is this responsibility?

The belayer must be in a safe and well-chosen location. In case of a fall, the strong pull on the rope must be sustained by the belayer. The belay position must provide a good stance so that the belayer can absorb such a load without being upset, thrown, rolled over, or even pulled from his belay position. This can be done by sitting down and straddling a rock or large tree. The belayer keeps the rope from fouling and out of the climber's way by anticipating his movements.

The belayer must also keep the rope clear and ready to be paid out. He must see to it that you have just enough rope for climbing and no more in order to reduce to a minimum the distance of a potential fall. If you do fall the belayer must hold the rope so that you stay where you are. The belayer then lowers you slowly either to the ground or to where you can regain your footing on the cliff. It is essential, therefore, that the belayer thoroughly understands the process involved, for when a climber falls several things happen almost instantaneously—there is no time for thinking, and *no* second chance.

The procedure required to protect both the belayer and the climber have been well outlined by instructors of the M.I.T. Outing Club as follows:

1. The belayer is tied from his waist loop to a tree, rock, piton, or similar secure object. There should be no slack in the tie-in rope.

2. The belayer is seated, preferably in a position where he can watch the climber.

3. The rope from the climber passes around the belayer's waist *above* the tie-in rope, and, after having passed around the belayer's waist, is held fast on the side away from the climber.

4. The belayer's hand is used to guide the rope and to sense the movements of the climber when he is not visible. The other hand is used to hold the rope. It must be on the rope at all times, and where it can clamp and hold effectively and immediately. The section of the rope having passed around the belayer's waist must always be held tight.

HERE IS AN excellent belay position. The belayer
sits securely in rock saddle, with solid bracing
of left foot. Ideally, his other boot sole
should also be placed against the rock. The metal
ring (called a carabiner) prevents rope being
injured by rock. (*Colorado Outward Bound School*)

AN ADEQUATE belay position. Fortunately, the belayer has most of his body weight in the back of the rock, and one boot braced against a crack. (*University of Colorado*)

AN EXTREMELY poor belay position.
The belayer standing on top could easily
be pulled off his perch by a falling climber.
Sitting is best for the belayer,
and if he must stand, he should himself
be anchored by means
of a rope and hardware.
(*Canadian Govt. Tourist Office*)

5. In case of a fall, the hand on the side of the body away from the climber, the braking hand, holds the fall. Only a very small force is necessary because the friction around the body absorbs most of the force from the fall.

6. Many times it will be found convenient to pass the rope around a tree or some other suitable object behind the belayer instead of around the belayer's waist, thereby taking the force of a fall off of his waist. Care should be taken to ensure that this is a smooth surface that will neither cut nor snag the rope. The rope-handling procedure is the same, and a tie-in is still necessary.

7. If either the climber or the belayer desires, a test of the belay may be made in a manner safe to both, but ultimately with the full weight of the climber on the rope.

Sometimes the belayer is hidden behind a rock and can't see you. But even if he can't, he's in touch with you—and you with him—by means of shouted signals. This way, you can make no mistakes. But voices must be strong and clear.

The signals are as follows:

CLIMBER: "Belay on?"
BELAYER: (*When ready*) "Belay on!" or "Belay *not* ready," so that climber knows signal was heard.
CLIMBER: "Testing."
BELAYER: (*When ready*) "Test." Climber applies jerk to indicate direction in which pull would occur.
CLIMBER: "Ready to climb."
BELAYER: "Climb!"
CLIMBER: (*As needed*) "Up rope," or "Slack."
BELAYER: (*As needed*) "Twenty-five feet," "Ten feet."
CLIMBER: (*When arrived and secure*) "Off belay."
BELAYER: (*Confirming*) "Belay *off*."
BOTH: (*In case of falling rock*) "ROCK!"

CLIMBER: (*In precarious position, if needed*) "Tension."
            (*If in doubt*) "Prepare for fall."
            (*Or if it happens!*) "Falling."

If the belayer needs to alter his position or his belay becomes insecure:

BELAYER: (*At the right moment*) "Belay *off*."
            (*Wait for answer*)
CLIMBER: (*Confirming*) "Off belay."
BELAYER: (*When ready*) "Belay on."

Naturally, the belay, like all roped climbing, requires rope skills, including the proper knots.

Some novice climbers can scoot up some awful pitches with the grace and smoothness and power of tigers yet have trouble with their knots—the knots that tie them into the rope, the knots that are needed to tie two ropes together, and the knots of their small sling ropes, which may well get the tigers out of a difficult situation. Unfortunately, knotting (like rifle cleaning or knitting) takes special aptitude. It also takes practice—a lot of practice for the untalented, and just a little for those with a mechanical bent. At first the tremendous variety of knots may be mysterious for all. One military instructor swears that you must know at least ten different ones before you can dare the granite boulder at the edge of town. To add further chaos, you will find that each guide has his own favorite knots.

The best way to learn knots is by watching an instructor. You can look up the "bowline" in any Boy Scout manual; it's standard. The bowline is for the first and last man. This knot is easy to tie, and it comes out easily when you release the tension, but not when you fall. In fact, you can put tremendous strain on the bowline. It's so strong that it held when a fellow towed a car to a garage with it! You'll find the

LET AN INSTRUCTOR show you the bowline. It's a simple knot
that holds the rope to your waist while you climb.
You form a loop (see A) and swing the free rope end into
the loop from below. The rope swings once around
the topmost rope section, then dives once more through
the loop (see B). Accuracy is important.
Other rope knots are too complicated to show here.
Let your instructor demonstrate them!

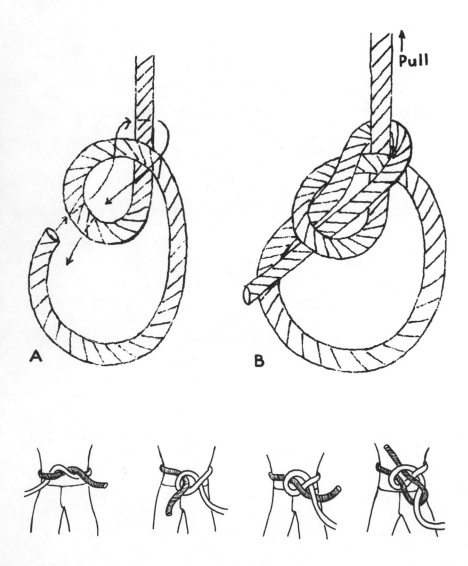

bowline unbeatable. To make a bowline, instructors often speak of "rabbits" and "holes." They'll ask you to form a loop and swing the free end of your rope through the loop from below (that's "the hole"). The rope then goes around the topmost and starting part ("around the tree") and swings through the hole a second time. And out of it. Bowline finished.

If you coil the rope a few extra times around your stomach, you have a so-called bowline-on-the-coil. This creates an extra shock absorber if you should ever fall and then hang free.

An instructor or a friend will at first help you with all these rope tricks. But remember that the rope must be tight at all times. An example of what can happen with a loose rope is the young man who fell into a Mt. Rainier crevasse. When his friends pulled him out, he coughed terribly. What had happened? The not-tight-enough rope had slipped from his waist to under his shoulders, pulling up shirt, undershirt, parka. And half-crazed with the cold in the crevasse, the boy was unable to pull the clothes over the tangled rope!

In fact, mountaineering annals are full of cases when comfort-demanding gents who preferred a slack rope around their midriff learned their lesson too late. A fall then pulled the ropes over their stout stomachs, over their thinning chests, over their arms, and finally over their heads. And down they went!

Once you've knotted your rope and then, for some reason, have stepped out of it, always put it back over your head. Don't step *into* it. And never step *on* your rope either. Treat the nylon with great care. And learn to coil it properly. There are several ways to do this. One widely accepted method is taught by the Outward Bound Schools. It goes like this: Start from the inside of the left leg, leaving the end hanging down. Bring the rope over the knee to the outside, around the foot to the inside. Continue in this manner, forming uniform loops, until the rope is completely coiled. The rope must always be coiled in a clockwise direction. If there is a tendency for the rope to twist or form figure eights it may be given a slight twist with the right hand to overcome this.

In finishing off the "mountain coil" make a foot-long bight (or loop) at the starting end of the rope to be laid along the top of the coil. Uncoil the last loop and take the length of rope thus formed and wrap it around the coil and the bight. Make the first wrap at the open end of the bight to lock it. Then continue wrapping toward the closed end until just enough rope remains to insert through the bight. Pull the running end of the bight to secure the wrapped rope. A rope properly coiled has from six to eight wraps.

To undo a coil, take off the rope loop by loop and then run the whole length back through your hands, inspecting it before use.

To most climbers the most thrilling rock maneuver is the rappel. It allows you to get down any cliff, no matter how slick or steep, by means of a rope. And in record time. The speed of the rappel is important when bad weather threatens, or when you want to do a lot of climbing in good weather. Instructors teach it by taking you first to an easy slab of perhaps forty-five degrees. Actually, just the first step takes courage. It is awkward because you step downward, with your back to the sky.

There are several types of rappels. The easiest one to learn, as taught by the M.I.T. Outing Club, goes like this: Pass the rope around a tree or similar solid object with no sharp corners (the anchor). Make certain that the rope cannot slip off. Throw both ends of the rope off the cliff and make sure that they both reach the bottom. Stand between the anchor and the cliff, and face the anchor. Pass the doubled rope

THIS YOUNG CLIMBER carefully ties his bowline knot before climbing. Note the slick, tear-shaped pack, ideal for climbing. (*Colorado Outdoor Sports Corp.*)

THIS CLIMBER carries an extra rope — well-coiled — around his shoulders. Good coiling results from use of foot and knee. Let an instructor show how it's done. (*University of Colorado*)

CLIMBERS jokingly call this a rope salad.
(*Colorado Outward Bound School*)

The "RAPPEL" enables a climber to get down any rock face.

(Opposite) THIS IS CALLED the free rappel. It is a little
bit like parachuting, and the lack of contact
with rock can be frightening at first. (*Stowe News Bureau*)

THE FIRST STEP of a rappel is always the
hardest—you have to go backward into the void.
Shortly, the belayer will sit down in the standard
belay position. (*Swiss National Tourist Office*)

between the legs from the front, under the right thigh, across the chest, over the left shoulder, diagonally across the back, and hold it with the right hand near the right thigh. (This may also be done left-handed; the check on the rappel is that the rope is always held in the hand on the opposite side from the shoulder it crosses.) Now lean back over the edge of the cliff and keep a tight grip on the rope with the right hand. The left hand holds the rope loosely before it passes between the legs and acts as a balance and guide. Keep the feet well apart, the legs straight, and the body about perpendicular to the cliff face. Now walk downward. It is a good idea to turn slightly so that you can see where you are going and where your rope is. Let the rope slide through the right hand to move down, clamp the rope tightly with the right hand to stop all motion. The left hand should not be used to support your weight at any time. If you have any difficulties, clamp down on the rope with the right hand, not the left hand.

This is easy to describe, but there are many problems the beginner must learn to avoid. It is recommended that you watch a demonstration first, and, when rappelling, always make sure you are belayed. It is advisable to wear extra-heavy clothing, or to have large patches sewn on your climbing outfit on the underside of the thigh and on the opposite shoulder. Do not wear nylon clothes when rappelling—nylon rubbed on nylon heats and fuses very rapidly. Also, going down in great leaps and stopping suddenly is very thrilling, but the tension developed in the rope during such antics can be exceedingly high and ropes have snapped under just such circumstances. Swinging from side to side is another poor practice because the rope may be pulled across sharp edges and severely cut.

Mistakes can trip you up on a rappel. Just a loose shirt can be dangerous. An experienced Utah climber still remembers a rugged experience in the Wasatch Range. "That afternoon we hit bad weather," he recalls. "Black clouds churned over-head. The sky rumbled with thunder a few miles away. Then the first drops fell. Soon bolts of lightning lit over our head. We *had* to rappel. And fast. So we were in an awful hurry. We were silly. Not even time for a belay. I went first. And about three-quarters of the way down, it happened. My shirt got mixed up in the rope. I was locked in! I had a knife around my belt. The blade was sharp and I tried to cut the shirt loose. The next thing I knew I had cut the rope by mistake! Not all the way. It held for another twenty feet down. Then all at once, rip! And crash! I went sailing to the platform below. Feet first. Almost incredibly, this got me just a sprained left ankle. But I'll get my shirt *in* from now on. . . ."

In the rappel, another problem often comes up. It's the matter of insufficient rope. If both ends do not reach the bottom, *never* attempt a rappel.

Most climbing accidents happen in rappelling. Needlessly.

The wisest word may have been spoken by Harold "Pop" Sorensen, a civilian who spent his lifetime as climbing instructor to the military. "The rappel isn't a game," Sorensen warns. "It's for real."

8 gear:
the well-equipped
mountaineer in action

Ropes

Climbing ropes are always furnished by mountaineering schools, and by many clubs that teach climbing. If you climb with a mountain guide, he, too will have his own rope. And lastly, if you join some other fellows—experienced ones!— for a rock ascent, the *leader* has a rope along. All of which means that at first you need not invest in one.

Eventually, though, you will become skilled enough to lead, and you will need your own rope. Modern climbing ropes are usually 120 feet long; a few (for long rappels) come in 150-foot sizes. In general, the diameters are ⁷⁄₁₆ or ⅜ of an inch. If a rope is smaller than that, it is hard to grasp and hold. (A national park ranger in Colorado once caught several boys trying to use a narrow clothesline!) Most North American climbers swear by nylon. In Europe, climbers prefer another synthetic fiber. This is *perlon*, and you'll find it available in some U.S. mountaineering stores. In the old days, before we had synthetic fibers, hemp was the material for ropes. But it was not very strong, aged fast when wet, and had to be replaced every year. Worse, hemp does not "give" and a rope should be elastic enough to absorb the weight of a falling climber. Nylon is very supple and at the same time it lasts a long time. A modern rope won't break even when four thousand pounds or more are suspended from it. Yet it is not heavy, and the price isn't high, either. The typical line of ropes might look like this:

Size	Average Breaking Strength	Approx. Weight	Price
7⁄16″ × 120′	5,500 lb.	6¼ lb.	$24.00
3⁄8 × 120	4,000	4½	16.00
7⁄16 × 150	5,500	7¾	29.00

A rope must be treated with care. It is a good idea to check it regularly for nicks, cuts, or badly frayed spots; also to see if it has come undone. Keep it away from fires and do not step on its fibers.

When you buy a rope, make sure that it's really new. You just can't have faith in secondhand ropes. The latter may have been treated badly by previous owners. If they were careless, strands may have been damaged by sharp rocks. The rope fibers could have been exposed to excessive heat or moisture. A bargain-priced secondhand rope is not a bargain at all.

Pitons

Pitons are spikes with closed loops on the end. You drive them into rock cracks in places too steep to climb unaided. Carabiners, which we will describe shortly, snap onto the loops and the rope goes through the carabiners. This is the basic system of rock climbing.

Pitons can be made of many different materials. The newest pitons, of special alloys and chrome-molybdenum and of carbon tool steels, are so much better than the old spikes that they are worth the extra cost. The extra strength can be vitally important. The choice of piton sizes has increased in recent years, and there is now one for every crack.

IT IS A GOOD IDEA to inspect ropes every time
you use them. Your life may depend on it.

Technical rock climbing can be as exciting as free climbing. Watch a rope of expert climbers moving up a vertical wall, placing and removing one hundred pitons a day, belaying and sleeping in hammocks hanging from these pitons. Watch the leader judge the size of a crack, glance down at his hardware loop, and without hesitation pick the correct-size piton and drive it in just enough to safely support his weight, clip in the carabiners and rope with no mistakes, and move up with the same fluid motion as the free climber. You cannot deny that this is indeed a well-developed form of art.

To become this good takes a great deal of practice. It also takes knowledge to select the right piton. Among the two dozen available types, here are some important ones, with data:

Model	Thickness	Total Length	Weight
½ ″	½ ″	4″	2 oz.
⅝	⅝	4 ¼	2 ½
¾	¾	5 ¾	3
1	1	5 ¾	3 ¾
1 ¼	1 ¼	6	5
1 ½	1 ½	6	6

How do you know which piton to use for the right spot? Keep two things in mind: First of all, the piton should have approximately the same shape as the crack. Second, it must fit at least one-third to one-half of the way into the crack before being driven with the hammer. For horizontal cracks use angles, horizontals, and wedges. For vertical cracks use verticals, wafers, and sometimes angles or other horizontal-type pitons.

When you feel that you need a piton, put one in. When climbing a vertical pitch, you should have a piton every ten to fifteen feet. Often you will be climbing a known route

HERE'S A NICE ASSORTMENT of large and small pitons and a piton hammer. The quality of such hardware has reached new heights in the United States. (*Tom Frost, Chouinard Co.*)

with pitons already in place. Each of these pitons should be thoroughly checked and, if necessary, taken out and redriven or replaced. Also, just because someone else has climbed there and put in pitons does not mean that all the necessary pitons are in.

How do you place a piton? There are really four steps:

1. Find the best place for a piton.
2. Select the right piton.
3. Drive the piton.
4. Test the piton.

In picking the place for a piton, several questions should be answered. One: Is it the place that will hold the piton most securely? Doubtful rock should be tapped with the hammer; a hollow or dead sound indicates an insecure section. If possible, choose a place where the piton can be driven at a sharp angle against the expected direction of pull in case of a fall. Two: Is it the place that will add the least rope friction to the system? Avoid setting pitons either way off to one side or back in corners, since this bends the rope and might drag it around corners. (Also be sure that the rope will be kept out of cracks where it could jam.)

Drive the piton straight. Repeated bendings can weaken it. Experienced mountaineers always listen to the sound of the piton while driving. It should have a rising tone to indicate proper tightening. A sudden drop in tone indicates a loosening of the piton, probably because of enlargement of the crack. Select a new spot and start over.

Remember, too, that when a piton is driven, only the eye or ring of the piton should remain outside of the crack.

According to the country's foremost authority on piton-craft, Yvon Chouinard, of Ventura, California, you should consider many other matters. Chouinard has observed, for example, that young climbers often "overdrive" their pitons.

The best alloy holding power comes not from hammering hard but from sophisticated placing, so that under a load the pitons will wedge themselves. The proper method is to begin by finding the section of crack that best fits the piton and provides natural resistance to shifting. Ideally the crack should grip the piton near both edges of the blade. If only a single high spot in the crack contacts the blade it can become an unwanted pivot point.

The piton size should normally allow half to three-quarters of the blade length, depending on piton size and taper, to be inserted into the selected section of the crack before driving. Pound the piton in only partway. Then test with a light downward blow on the head to see how well it is in and how well it resists shifting. If it is all right, then drive some more and retest with another downward blow until the piton appears very solid in its resistance to shifting. Restrain the urge to give it that one extra blow—this is the one that will make the piton difficult to remove. If, however, a perfect placement is not possible, then the best security can be obtained, particularly in vertical cracks, from a really hard-driven piton.

A perfect placement is one where a piton can be inserted with the fingers plus one hammer blow and hold four thousand pounds. It is important to remember that every single piton must be tested before use. You do this by hitting the piton once or twice sideways and observing if it shifts in the crack. Any old piton left in place must be tested in the same way. When driving more than one piton, make sure the second piton has not expanded the crack and allowed the first to loosen.

Chouinard suggests using shorter-length pitons in a very crooked crack, such as you may find in some limestone. And never use a blade-type piton which is bent over forty-five degrees.

You must also employ the right technique when removing pitons. Novice climbers often make the mistake of not hitting the spikes far enough in each direction, but rather just back and forth a little way. The proper method is to hit the piton in one direction until it absolutely will go no farther —then drive it back in the opposite direction. But be sure to stop before the piton starts deforming. To avoid deforming the head, direct removal blows to the neck areas rather than the anvil of the piton.

A piton that cannot be removed indicates it was over-driven, poorly placed, or the remover has insufficient experience. Climbs have been done in Yosemite where 450 pitons have been placed and all but 2 or 3 were taken out.

In many years of testing various types of pitons, Chouinard has discovered some additional pointers. Among them:

• Pitons of alloy steel can be considered safer because its holding power is greater than that of soft steel. Tests have shown that the average pullout load for soft pitons in horizontal cracks in hard rock is less than 1,500 pounds; whereas the average pullout load for alloy steel pitons under identical conditions is in excess of 4,000 pounds.

• Pitons of alloy steel rust faster than those of steel or iron. For this reason keep your pitons in a dry place.

• Alloy pitons wear out differently from soft pitons. Rather than becoming unrecognizable blobs of bent iron, they keep their shape for a long time, sometimes for a hundred uses, but when fatigue cracks develop— usually at the junction of the eye and the blade, along their length—the pitons should be discarded.

• Angle pitons serve a long time because of their rigidity. Although light in weight, the one-half–inch wedge fits the very common wedge-size cracks found in granite.

Carabiners

The carabiner is the link between your piton and the rope. You need not worry about many varieties, for almost all 'biners (also called snap links) have an oval shape. They are made of steel or aluminum, and most of them have "gates" that connect with the piton eye and also with rope.

Carabiners *must* be placed correctly to be of real value. They should have their gate *away* from the cliff so that they cannot be forced open by the rock during a fall. The gate opening should be at the lower end of the carabiner. In this position, it will allow the snapping in or out of the rope. Since your life (and that of your companions) depends on carabiners, you must check them before every climb.

A sticky gate in a carabiner might be caused by a blow from a hammer. In that case, look for a small burr on the gate and file it off. Do not use oil on the gates, because it attracts dirt and will eventually clog up the gate.

Unless the gates work perfectly, they are useless and dangerous. The same applies to the metal "lock sleeve" which protects the gate of some snap links. Test this sleeve before trusting your weight to it.

Defective carabiners have meant disaster to a number of climbers. Test every one before each use.

The use of carabiners and the right employment of pitons brings great satisfactions, because walls can be scaled that could not be handled at all without this hardware.

Still, the pounding of pitons and this sort of rope work should *never* be attempted by a beginner. You need a real expert along. Most major mountaineering accidents happen to untried, untrained amateurs who are unfamiliar with the technique.

The leader on a climb is belayed only by climbers *below* himself. If he slips, he will fall until the rope is taut at the last

THE CARABINER (nicknamed "biner") is also called
a snaplink from the snapping shut of the gate,
which you see on top of the biner. (*Tom Frost, Chouinard Co.*)

piton he placed. So after each upward inch, he must ask himself: Do I need a piton now? The farther he gets away from the belayer below, the more essential becomes piton placement. The pitons should be in a straight, vertical line; this way, the rope will run smoothly between the leader and the belayer. Don't let any kinks develop in the rope, and don't allow it to scrape on rock.

Remember, too, that with the employment of hardware, only *one* man in your party can move at one time, while the other people on the team wait. Normally, the last man removes the pitons.

Mountaineering with the help of pitons and carabiners is a joy, despite its slowness. Fortunately, your descent can be accomplished much faster. You use the rappel.

9 inside story:
avoiding the dangers

Mountaineering is a safe sport if you know what you're doing. Only a few climbers suffer serious injuries. Fatalities are rare. This is borne out by the yearly accident report of the American Alpine Club. During a typical year, less than one hundred people are involved in mountain mishaps. Of these, 80 per cent are just injuries.

Nearly all hazards can be avoided by staying with a group and using common sense. Without caution, you can get over-tired, and at higher elevations, you can get sunburned unless you use zinc oxide or another screening agent. In the West, an occasional hiker has fallen into an old mine shaft, or after racing down a trail, tumbled down the mountainside. None of these accidents need occur.

Common sense begins with proper attire. One Colorado hiker ventured onto a steep snow-field in tennis shoes. While frolicking, he started to slide and was finally and fatally stopped by rocks. Two young people, both in shorts, tried to ascend Mount Washington, New Hampshire, in midsummer. An unexpected snowstorm surprised them, and they died unnecessarily just a few steps away from a hut. The cold had been just too much for scanty attire.

Short-sleeved shirts plus light summer pants are just not

sufficient in the mountains. Keep in mind that at higher altitudes, weather can be exceedingly changeable. Even in midsummer the temperature above nine thousand feet can be freezing despite warm conditions below. Always bring wind-resistant and water-resistant warm clothing. An extra sweater is advisable for emergency use. Mittens, sunglasses, and hat are essential.

Mountain weather is capricious. It's best not to attempt a major high-altitude hike in poor weather. Weather conditions leading to complete whiteout even in midsummer can spell hardship to the most experienced groups on the treeless slopes above timberline. What may have started as a pleasant alpine stroll in sunshine can end as a miserable experience due to the changeable weather. Fortunately, there are certain indicators:

- Red sunsets or sunrises and rainbows can mean high humidity in the area. This could result in rain, particularly if located to the west.
- Yellow sunsets or sunrises are indicators of low humidity.
- A small ring around the sun or the moon, called a "corona," and the much larger ring, called a "halo," are caused by moisture in the air and are signs of a coming *or* departing disturbance.
- The sound of thunder is a warning that a disturbance is in progress. If lightning is visible you may be able to estimate the distance of the disturbance. Count the seconds between lightning and thunder. Each second means about a mile's distance from the thunderstorm. Remember that it's no disgrace to turn back from a mountain, or to seek shelter.

Lightning in the mountains can be dangerous. Stay off high, exposed points and ridges during electrical storms. Knowing something of the environment will prevent most trouble. For instance, you should never seek the shelter of a lone tree, or stand under a rock overhang or next to rock spires. Strangely enough, cave entrances are also bad protection when lightning strikes. You're best off at the foot of a cliff which is five or ten times your height. Spread out your knapsacks, or rubberized rain jackets or ponchos (folded several times). Then squat on these insulators. Do not make yourself a "lightning rod"; stay away from any metal you are carrying.

If you're hiking in rocky terrain, avoid chimneys or tight gullies (these are known as couloirs). If lightning smashes into a summit, stones and boulders may start cascading down these gullies. Rocks can also become dislodged during a warming trend and *after* thundershowers.

Only highly skilled and fully equipped groups should consider a winter ascent. Even the brilliant sunshine of a January day can turn into a nightmare of the arctic wastelands in an hour's time. In winter, conditions above timberline are comparable to those in arctic areas. Winter climbing must be reserved for the experienced. In certain high regions, such as the U.S. Northwest, and in some Canadian areas, snow and ice last all year.

Only tourists and children are foolish enough to brave snow fields or glaciers *alone*. Luck is sometimes with them. An unequipped loner once broke through a crevasse, which is a crack in the ice. After trying to hang on, he fell thirty feet, landed in one piece, and shouted. For two days, a dozen people went past and didn't hear him from the depth of his icy shaft. Then the shouting ceased. The man waited. He hadn't told anyone about this journey. Fortunately for him, a guide striding past the fissure noticed that the edges showed traces of frantic struggles and discovered the loner. The tourist was pulled out alive, but he was much less adventurous thereafter.

As a hiker in the West, you may also be faced by the

BEFORE LIGHTNING strikes, avoid standing under an overhang
or on an exposed summit. Your best place is down
in the valley or at the foot of a cliff many times your height.
(*Vermont Development Dept.*)

possibility of avalanches. In Colorado, for instance, snow masses can roar down a mountainside as late as June. And because there can still be snowstorms in Montana and Wyoming during the month of May, you should know something about avalanche hazards. Remember that snowslides have enormous destructive power. So if you must hike up in snowy terrain, plan your route well. Avoid steepness. Avoid gullies or slopes where trees have been wiped out. What do you do if caught in an avalanche? First of all, call out. Second, try to stay on the surface using a swimming motion, and try to move to one side of the crushing snow. Cover your face with your hands. This will help keep snow out of your mouth, and you will have a chance to clear a breathing space if you are buried. Avalanche snow often becomes very hard as soon as it stops moving. Your arms may be pinned wherever you find them when the snow comes to rest. If you are buried, try to avoid panic. In soft snow you may be able to dig yourself out, or at least make room to breathe. Make sure you dig up toward the surface. Persons buried in an avalanche have lost their sense of direction and actually tried to dig down.

Don't waste your strength by shouting after you are buried. Sound is transmitted very poorly through snow.

Hikers even in flat, dry country must avoid the problem of getting lost. If you stay on the trail, or walk with experienced leaders, you seldom have to worry about this hazard. If you hike off a trail, you should look back once in a while. An early start also helps; it gives you a little extra time.

As a precaution, study a map of the area before venturing into it. Experienced backpackers frequently use rest stops to pinpoint on the map their positions on the ground. It is a good idea to practice using maps on strange short trails before starting the first real trip. Also practice following a straight line for a short distance through trailless country, using map and compass.

The compass is one of the "ten essentials." There are many varieties of a good, small pocket compass. The dial should not be smaller than 1½ inches in order to be reasonably accurate and easily readable. Be sure to familiarize yourself with your compass. It is the most reliable means of establishing the direction of north and it is usable under all conditions. One end of the compass needle always points to the magnetic north pole and should be distinguishable from the other end of the needle. The face of the compass is divided into 360 degrees. Starting with North as 0 degrees or 360 degrees and proceeding clockwise, East is 90 degrees, South is 180 degrees, and West, 270 degrees. Large iron-base metal objects, such as pack frames or hardware, should not be close to the compass when you set it up for use.

If a trail disappears and you have no compass, there is no reason to get excited. Stop, think, look. Pull out the map and get oriented by stream drainages or lakes. Backtrack if necessary. Follow broken twigs, bent grass, or overturned stones left en route.

If this still doesn't work, build a fire and keep it going. If the weather is good and a Forest Service lookout is on duty, he will send someone to investigate. Use green boughs to make a dense smoke and little flame. Keep the fire small.

How about signals? Distress signals come in three's. Three whistles, shouts, gunshots, three flashes of light, three smoke puffs, or three of anything that attracts attention means someone is in trouble. Avoid unnecessary noise or action that would indicate you are in trouble unless you are.

It is interesting to note how different people, including adults, face emergencies in different ways. Let's take a remote Alaskan highway, hundreds of miles from nowhere. A truck engine stalls; two truck drivers jump out and try to revive it. They frantically work all day. And fail. The penetrating cold changes to a blizzard. The two men have gasoline, food, sleeping bags, blankets, and strong bodies. Yet they go crazy with fear, and start marching into the wilderness—in search of help, which never comes.

On the other hand, a couple of pilots who crashed in savage country on a Wyoming peak managed to struggle back to civilization after living on toothpaste for three days.

It's all a matter of avoiding panic.

Safety experts also say that most *accidents are caused by either unsafe acts or unsafe conditions*. In the mountains many naturally unsafe conditions exist, such as cliffs, snowbanks, lakes, rivers, and rugged terrain, and all are part of the natural environment.

Among mountaineers, the hysterical, the nervous, the impatient, the thoughtless, and the dumb or overconfident all must pay a price. It takes experience and judgment to climb safely. Your gear will not ensure a safe climb unless you know how to use your tools. Good judgment might dictate turning back short of the summit when terrain or weather conditions are forbidding. Desire to reach a summit does not justify taking chances. When you take unnecessary risks and jeopardize your own safety, you may also be jeopardizing the safety of the others in your party and of teams which might come to your aid.

The causes of accidents have been analyzed and pinpointed by the Safety Committee of the American Alpine Club. Here, as seen by the AAC, are the reasons for mountaineering mishaps, in the order of their importance:

1. Fall or slip on rock.
2. Climbing unroped.
3. Slip on snow or ice.
4. Attempt to exceed ability, or inexperience.
5. Falling rock or object.
6. Climbing alone.

7. Failure of rappel.
8. Inadequate equipment (including old ropes).
9. Failure of piton.
10. Avalanche.
11. Climbing while tired, and exposure.
12. Lightning.
13. Climbing in darkness.

The greatest number of accidents happen when a climber uses only his feet and not his head. Overconfidence does not pay.

When a Colorado leader asked a seventeen-year-old to descend behind him the *easy* way, the boy smirked. "That's the long way round."

"Been down here before?" the leader asked.

"First time. But I have eyes. I want to go straight down."

The leader said sharply: "It isn't safe. And safety is all that counts."

The boy laughed out loud. Five minutes later, he wept. He'd fallen onto a ledge and broken four ribs.

In another incident a leader insisted on an easy route through the Rockies. But a boy challenged him. "I've climbed in Canada," he said. "I've done better than the eighty-nine hundred feet of the Twin Peaks. And I want to *climb* them now. No hikes for me!" The leader protested. It didn't help. The fellow struck out alone. Before long, he hit some rotten lava rock and fell.

Too much confidence cost the life of a mountaineer who had performed the most astonishing international climbing feats. Each expedition made him more daring. He chalked up victory after victory in the Rockies, the Andes, the Himalayas. One day he went to Russia. He was now so sure of himself that he didn't want to be belayed. "Let's make time," he told his equally famous rope partner. "Let's not stop." So they hurried up the Russian cliffs without rope security. All of a sudden both men plunged to their doom. And this after a lifetime of superb Alpinism.

Avoid mountaineering as competition. Every summer, groups race up the difficult Devils Tower in Wyoming, trying to see who makes it first. Or they hold a rock-climbing race on the Flatirons in Colorado. Or national teams try to beat each other to the summits of Swiss mountains. This is foolish. The intelligent climber doesn't compete with others. He should only struggle against nature and the elements and against his own weakness.

F. S. Smythe, a well-known climber-philosopher, puts it this way: "Competitive mountaineering breeds a callousness of outlook. Nature is outraged when an atmosphere of feverish human competition is introduced into her sanctuaries." Fearlessness coupled with heedlessness always spells hazards.

Rock climbers must be safety-conscious. Always use sound techniques. This includes a good belay whenever necessary. Check all items of equipment for wear and tear. If in doubt about a knot, ask someone. Forget the rappel unless you're familiar with an area. Get a hard hat as protection against falling rocks. (Fasten the chin strap tightly.) While free-climbing, test all handholds and footholds. In short, assume nothing. And never be afraid to turn back. The mountain will still be there when you return. Remember that you must always have a safety margin. That is why many mountaineers start out at dawn. It gives them extra time for the unforeseen and for a cautious descent.

Make sure to plan your route down as you are climbing up. Will you be able to get *down* where you went up? The descent is always more difficult, and if you're not sure that you can make it safely, you'll have to choose an easier route. Always realize your limitations. If you're in charge, you must do more than just please yourself. You must pick the

SOME PEOPLE ALSO come to harm in the mountains.
This old etching shows some troubles on the
Matterhorn, in Switzerland. (*Swiss National Tourist Office*)

way best suited to the *entire* party. Route selection is a difficult job and experience is the best teacher. A beginner tends to rate routes easier than they really are when inspecting them from a distance. If you do this and find yourself on a climb beyond the capabilities of your party or on a climb that is going to take too long, don't hesitate to come back down.

Come what may, a party must stay together. It is a mistake to separate. In a well-publicized climb of Mount Adams, Washington, a group of nine ropeless climbers fanned out over the peak. Soon a fog engulfed them. Then fifty-mile-per-hour gusts of wind began. In time, without consulting anyone, several climbers returned to base camp. The others frantically searched for one another in the fog and storm. One man was left on the mountain during the night. When his companions finally found him, it was too late.

Climbing alone is even more dangerous. A simple emergency can be handled by a group with little effort but may be the undoing of a lone climber. Three should be the minimum number in a climbing party. With this number, one climber can stay with an injured person while another goes for help; or two can always more adequately assist an injured or fatigued member of the group.

On some U.S. mountains "solo" climbing is actually forbidden. In the Grand Teton National Park, for instance, this is one of the posted rules: "No person shall climb alone on rock, snow, or ice regardless of location. This also means that parties must not leave one member alone at any time while climbing."

In all national parks, climbers must sign in at the ranger stations, and then sign out again when they return. This is certainly a good idea in all areas. In some cities, like Boulder, Colorado, rescue groups set up a "mountaineering register." Before starting out, any climber can call a switchboard telling the operator where he is going and when he intends to get back. If he hasn't returned by a certain time, the operator informs the rescuers. Unfortunately, not enough climbers take advantage of the register. In fact, climbers often don't tell *anybody* what they're up to!

Sometimes climbers sign out, but, heady with summit triumphs, don't bother to sign in. As a consequence, the rescue group may be searching all night for a young person who is in his own bed. This search can take on major proportions. One time, for example, the Boulder volunteer group drove its jeeps half the night looking for a missing climber. Thinking that the missing climber might have ventured onto one of the high peaks, they mobilized helicopters. All for nothing. The fellow had driven back to his home. He just forgot to call!

None of these regulations and precautions should keep you from climbing, however. Some cragsmen have been at it all their lives, without a scratch. Take the case of Glenn Exum, chief guide at the Teton National Park Mountaineering School. Exum is a minor god in the annals of American Alpinism. He taught four Everest climbers and created dozens of our most important guides. Safety-conscious to the extreme, *Exum's school has led some ten thousand climbers through the Tetons in the past twenty-five years without a single major accident!*

10 aftermath: rescues and first aid

You can hike and climb for a lifetime without ever facing an emergency. Yet when a mishap happens, you must know the right things to do.

One of the best ways to prepare for emergencies is to enroll in an American Red Cross first-aid course. They are given free in some 3,300 American Red Cross chapters all over the U.S. Among many other things, the course will introduce you to first-aid kits, which should be carried on rock-climbing ventures. You can make up a first-aid box by buying the supplies one by one (see below), or you can get a prepackaged kit at a drugstore.

Here are the essential items:

- 6 adhesive bands
- 1 two-inch "Ice" bandage
- 1 or 2 triangular bandages
- 6 three-inch-square sterile gauze pads
- 1 two-inch roller gauze bandage
- 5 or 10 yards of one-inch non-waterproof adhesive tape
- 2 two-inch compress bandages with tails
- 1 four-inch compress bandage with tails

1 small container (not glass) of an antibiotic or a pet-
rolatum ointment (for burns)
Aspirin tablets (about 12)
Single-edge razor blade

Bandages and other items are not much good until you learn
to use them properly. And you need to be shown how to apply artificial respiration and how to handle the many types
of fractures. You will learn all this in the course as well as
these established first-aid principles:

- Keep the injured person quiet, warm, and comforta-
ble.
- Loosen tight clothing such as collar, waistband, and
belt.
- Work fast, but carefully.
- Obtain medical aid quickly.
- Avoid letting the injured see his own injury, and in
severe cases do not let him know how badly he is hurt.
- Always treat the most dangerous condition first: for
example, stop bleeding before attending to a fracture.

Some don'ts:

- Don't attempt to give an unconscious person anything to drink.
- Don't touch a wound with your fingers.
- Don't burn the injured person with an unwrapped
hot-water bottle or other heated object.
- Don't allow the injured person with a fracture or
suspected fracture to be moved until splints have been
applied.
- Do not aggravate injury by unnecessary movements.

Dr. Hans Kraus, a well-known mountaineering physician,
has this to add: "A young person meeting a severe accident
for the first time should remain calm, should not be shocked

MOUNTAINEERING accidents are never a pleasant sight.
Keep your nerve, and practice the first-aid rules. (*Gordon Mansell*)

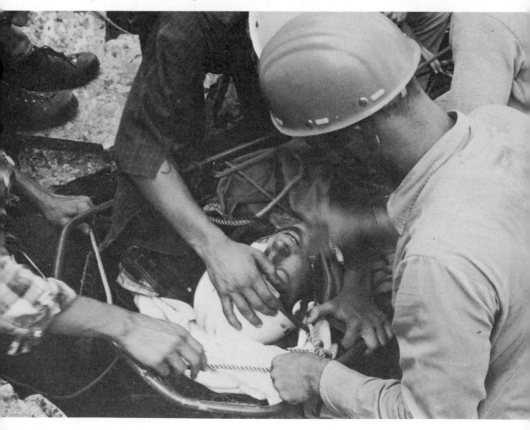

by seeing blood, and should not jump to any hasty and frantic action."

Small wounds can be cleansed with soap and water, and dressed with sterile gauze. Wounds with severe bleeding should be taken care of by the most experienced person in your group. If you're the only person with the victim, you'll have to apply firm pressure on the wound with gauze pack to control bleeding. If blood still spurts, apply additional pressure. For foot, leg, or thigh wounds, apply pressure in the middle of the groin with the heel of your hand. For hand, forearm, or arms, apply pressure on the inner side of the arm above the elbow. For neck, face, or scalp, keep firm pressure on the wound itself.

Bandaging is an art, and the American Red Cross devotes several hours to teaching it.

The same goes for splinting of fractured bones. Remember that you must keep the patient *flat* if the legs, back, or neck are injured. If you happen to be a junior National Ski Patrol member, you've already learned how to splint. You'll know that splints can be improvised from any handy material such as padded boards, pillows, blanket, newspapers. Wood splints are easiest to handle. They should be long enough to reach beyond the joints above and below the fracture, and should always be well padded. Put splints on each side of the limb and bandage them with the limb in between. For padding, absorbent cotton is the best material. To improvise padding use soft cloth or a soft garment. For binding, use the triangular or roller bandage or handkerchiefs, towels, tape, suspenders, straps, or adhesive plaster. Never transport a victim until splinted!

There is always the possibility of "shock" after a mountaineering accident. Shock can cause falling temperature, so make sure that the victim is stretched out on something dry and warm such as a blanket. And cover him well.

In the higher mountains, even during the summer, you

may have to cope with frostbite. Many medical papers have been written about this subject. Be aware that frostbite can occur at above-freezing temperatures, especially if it's windy. Hands can be thawed by placing them in your armpits; ears by covering them with hands. Never rub the affected area; never put it near a fire or use snow. Forget all about *hot* water; the best remedy is lukewarm water. In many cases, the use of a sleeping bag also helps. Avoiding frostbite is one reason for carrying a pair of mittens on high-country hikes and climbs. Advanced rock climbers also need mittens because rope friction can cause rope burn.

In cold weather, pitons sometimes create situations that require first aid. If you touch freezing metal with bare hands, you can get blisters. Your hand might even become frozen to metal. Pull it off gradually but waste no time in getting started. The longer you're stuck, the deeper it freezes. Also be careful with pots and pans during a blizzard.

If you live in a flat state like Nebraska, Kansas, Louisiana, or in the Canadian plains, there is always the chance of mountain sickness when you venture into the high country. You can avoid this sickness (its symptoms: nausea and exhaustion) by spending a few quiet days in the peaks before attempting any climbs. Then, when you're used to the altitude, you can undertake more strenuous things. For those in poor physical condition, the risk of getting sick is greater. Headaches, loss of appetite, and irritability might be signals of mountain sickness. Get some rest. Eat often but lightly. If nothing helps, return to a lower elevation, then try again. Mountaineers say that it takes one day to get used to each thousand feet, meaning that you'll have to be in the Rockies two weeks to climb a fourteen-thousand-footer. Some people get "acclimatized" much sooner, though.

There may be occasions when you have to dispense pills to someone who is sick or hurt. Be sure you give the proper kind. To avoid giving the wrong drugs, it is essential that you *mark* all drugs in your first-aid kit.

Following an accident, attention should be given to the safety of the whole party. In many cases the place of an accident is not the safest or best place to leave a victim. In looking for the best location you should consider safety, availability of water, protection from the elements, absence of rock falls, avalanches, and other immediate dangers, and accessibility to trails. When someone is injured, you'll have to give up your own plans, of course. It's a mountain code that you *must* give help. This means to another nearby party as well as your own. In some cases, such as a minor sprain or an arm wound, the injured person can get to safety on his own. (Always make sure that someone is with him all the way.) With more serious injuries, and with some kinds of minor ones, your companion may have to be transported down a mountain.

If there is a person strong enough to carry the injured person down, secure the patient with a rope to the person. The center of the rope is placed under the casualty's buttocks. The right loose end is passed under the carrier's right armpit, across his chest, over his left shoulder, and under the casualty's left arm. The left loose end is passed under the carrier's left armpit, across his chest, and over his right shoulder, under the casualty's arm, and the tie is made across his back. Use some padding against the rope.

If an accident takes place on a steep rock face or cliff, you may have no choice but to get the human package down. Use sound mountaineering principles. Lean away from the slope as much as possible. Walk sidewise, allowing a belay man to support you, rather than facing the slope and descending backwards. This can prevent unnecessary falls. By keeping your lower leg well braced, keeping the weight of the casualty high on your back, and by grasping trees and rocks, you can descend very steep slopes. On major expeditions, you may have a litter along. Or you can summon litter help from the nearest "mountain rescue" unit. (For addresses of mountain-rescue organizations, write *before* major climbs to: Mountain Rescue Association, P.O. Box 67, Seattle, Washington 98111.)

If you're many miles (or even days) away from assistance and an accident occurs, you may have to rig up an emergency litter yourself. According to the Outward Bound School in Maine, which teaches rescue work to young people, here is how you can improvise:

- The sapling litter is made by lashing together five or six saplings about seven or eight feet long. It can be padded with blankets or other clothing.
- The rope litter is made by running a climbing rope back and forth around a pole frame.
- The pole litter is made by wrapping a casualty in a blanket or canvas. This load is then suspended from a pole about fifteen feet long and three inches in diameter by means of a climbing rope passed around pole and person.
- A rope seat can easily be made from a coil of climbing rope, or about eighty feet of sling rope. Coil the rope loosely into fifteen-inch to twenty-inch coils. Do not tie the ends of the rope, but at one point tightly wrap around a handkerchief or a short string to keep the coils together. Divide the coil in two to make a seat for the victim. The rescuer carries the victim like a rucksack.
- A ski litter can be made from a pair of skis if you happen to be in snowy country and have skis along. Several skis bound together, covered with clothes, can also make a sled.
- Packboards or ice axes can be shaped into stretchers, too.

There are two additional hints to remember with all types of litters. First, a sleeping bag is ideal padding for the injured

LITTERS CAN BE improvised from saplings, trees, ropes, skis. (*U.S. Army*)

person. Second, make sure to *tie* the accident victim to the litter so he does not fall off.

Getting a man to safety (also called "evacuation") can be difficult in the high mountains. It's also very tiring. And it can be complex. There are advanced methods, which you can read about in books on the subject or learn from mountain rescue units. You might even want to join a volunteer mountain-rescue unit when you become an experienced climber.

Unless you are highly skilled in evacuation methods, you will have no choice but to get *outside* help as fast as possible for a serious accident. Here are some pointers on doing the correct thing. First of all, make sure that the messenger you send has *all* the information about the accident and the injured person. Rescue units must bring the proper equipment. If your party can spare them, two people should be sent to deliver the message. If the group is so small that only one can be spared, he should not travel by night, except under ideal conditions. According to the rescue specialists of the Sierra Club, a really effective message for help should have the following information in writing:

- Time and place of accident
- Nature of the injury
- Name and condition of the victim
- Number of people in assistance and their names
- Terrain over which evacuation must take place
- Special equipment or supplies necessary for rescue
- Details for notification of families of members in the party

The information should be delivered to state or federal park or forest rangers, to county sheriff's officers, to the state highway patrol, or to equivalent officers. These are the authorities most concerned with rescue organization and procedures and are the ones who can get in touch fast with mountain rescue units.

Once a rescue message has been delivered, preparations for rescue equipment are best left to local authorities. At this point, the mountaineer may be called upon as an advisor since he is still the only person who has firsthand knowledge of the situation.

A RESCUE being performed by Colorado Outward Bound rescue team. (*Colorado Outward Bound School*)

The party remaining with the victim meanwhile has the job of preparing for evacuation while caring for the injured. Mark the location so that it can be easily found by the rescue party. If you have had the foresight to bring a "survival kit" along, it should be in a waterproof bag and should contain these items:

> Emergency food (K ration or equal, plus one-quarter pound of chocolate or hard candy)
>
> Penny box of matches (not safety); fill with hot paraffin to waterproof
>
> Short plumber's candle (about four inches long), or other fire-making aids for use with wet wood or in adverse weather
>
> Fishline and flies
>
> Repair material (tape, wire, rivets, and cord)
>
> International ground-to-air rescue signals, Morse code, and any other information you feel necessary, on durable waterproof cards
>
> Metal signaling mirror
>
> Whistle

In the last few years, planes and helicopters have been used more in rescues. Naturally these are much faster than any ground party. Sometimes, though, wind and visibility make air rescues impossible. Remember that planes require a landing strip, fairly long, level, and free of obstructions, seldom available at higher elevations. Helicopters, at present, operate with reduced lift margin at higher altitude or over uneven ground.

On the ground you can be of help by preparing for possible overflights. A blazing fire is visible from great distances. Throwing water, wet logs, or green leaves on the fire causes a mixture of steam and smoke which is more visible than just the fire if you are near cliffs which block the direct line of sight. Before the first pass over the camp a test smoke signal should be produced to indicate the direction and intensity of the wind.

Both airplanes and helicopters have a system of replying "yes," "no," "message understood," and "not understood," and you should learn these.

Dipping of wing or rotor to
left *and* right . . . .   "Message understood"
Steep-banked close circle to
left *or* right. . . . .   "Message not understood"
Short dippings of bow of air-
craft . . . .   "Yes," affirmative
Short sideways skidding of
craft to left *and* right . . . .   "No," negative

The U.S. Coast Guard has adopted a set of sixteen international "ground-to-air" visual signals. They are used to communicate with an overflight. Ten of these signals are of importance to a land party and are reproduced below. They are simple enough.

International Ground-to-Air Visual Signals

I Require doctor   I I Require medical supplies

X Cannot proceed   F Require food and water

JL Not understood   ✓ Am proceeding this way

LL All well   △ Safe to land here

N No, negative   Y Yes, affirmative

To produce these ground signals, prepare the area ahead of time by clearing it of other objects. Prepare equipment to be used. Color contrast between signs and background is important. The size of the signs should be six to eight feet. Thus sleeping bags, liners, air mattresses, ground sheets, even individuals themselves may be used.

There are two rather rare situations—avalanches and falls into crevasses—that call for special rescue techniques.

If an avalanche comes down and you are the only survivor, the lives of your buried comrades may depend on what you do in the next hour. *Check for further slide danger* and pick a safe escape route in case of a repeat slide. Mark the point of the avalanche path where the victim was last seen as he was carried down by the snow. Next, make a quick but careful search of the surface of the avalanche for evidence of the victim or clues to his location. Mark the location of any pieces of equipment you may find for indications of the path taken by the flowing snow. Kick up the snow to uncover anything that may lie just beneath the surface.

If you are the *sole* survivor, you must still make a thorough search of the avalanche area before going for help. This may seem obvious, but it is a rule all too often neglected. Even the simplest search may enable you to find the victim and free him alive. If it will take many hours or longer to summon a rescue party, you must concentrate on making as thorough a search as possible with your own resources since the help would almost certainly come too late. The chances of a buried victim being recovered alive diminish after fifteen minutes.

If the initial search fails, begin probing with a ski, a ski pole, a probe pole, or a tree branch. Trees, ledges, benches, or other terrain features which have caught the snow should be probed first. Probing of likely spots can continue until a rescue party arrives. If you are alone, you will have to decide when to break off the effort and seek help, depending on how far away it is. If there are several survivors, send only two. Those remaining can search for the victim.

When going for help, travel carefully, avoiding more avalanche dangers. Mark your route so you can find your way back. The rescue party will normally expect you to guide them back to the accident scene.

Treat an avalanche victim immediately for suffocation and shock. Free his nose and mouth of snow and administer mouth-to-mouth artificial respiration if necessary. Clean snow from inside his clothing and place him in a sleeping bag with his head downhill. Any further injuries should then be treated according to standard first-aid practices.

The other special rescue situation to consider is a fall into the big, slitlike crevasses you find in glaciers. In the Alps, there are more than two thousand glaciers, and at one time all of Canada was covered by them. In Alaska the Hubbard Glacier still extends a distance of seventy-five miles. Many young mountaineers climb in the glaciated Pacific Northwest, especially on Mount Rainier. So a little information on crevasse emergencies can come in handy.

Should a climber fall into a crevasse, you'll have to get him out quickly because the ice inside of a crevasse chills the victim and increases the danger of severe shock. The importance of speed in the rescue makes it vital that every member of the party be trained in the details of rescue operation. Smooth, competent methods can, in a few minutes, save a life that might otherwise be lost.

If there is another climbing party in the vicinity, its help should be summoned in nearly every case of a crevasse fall. The added strength and additional equipment will increase the chances of a successful rescue.

Of course, before you go ahead, you must always know the situation *inside* the crevasse. For example, where firm masses of snow clog the crack some distance below the surface, it is easier to lower the victim to such a platform and begin rescue operations from there. In estimating the conditions within the crevasse, remember that a person even a short distance from the crevasse will find it almost impossible to hear the voice of the victim in the hole. Therefore, one member of the party, while belayed by another, must approach the hole to investigate.

Whether or not the victim is able to reach firm footing within the crevasse, the rescue procedure remains essentially the same. Spare rope should always be carried by a single rope party. If no spare ropes are available, as many members of the party as necessary will have to unrope to provide sufficient rope to reach the fallen man. The simplest and quickest procedure is to lower the loose end of this rope until he can reach it; it then is securely belayed on the surface. While he is being pulled up by this rope, he should be instructed to pull himself up on the anchored rope if possible.

A victim can be unconscious or too severely injured to give assistance. With enough people in the party, and if such a victim is light enough, he can simply be hauled out. If this is impossible, another climber might be lowered into the crevasse to remove the victim's pack, which could be pulled up separately; to give first aid; to put warm clothing on the victim; and to help pull the victim up.

Almost every accident can be prevented by proper learning and common sense. Rescue procedures should be learned "just in case." You may become involved in rescuing a member of your own party or even of another party who has been as careful as yourself.

11 lessons
and companions:
schools, clubs, camps

For instruction and to find companions, you might be interested in climbing clubs. There are such clubs, many with junior chapters, all over the country, and nearly all have teaching programs. What's more, you can join special outdoor camps during the summer or sign up for courses in mountaineering schools. In some regions you can even hire a guide who will teach you as you go along. In short, you have plenty of opportunities to get the right instruction and to make friends as well. The opportunities abound all over North America. Let's take a look at them, starting in the West.

One of the biggest organizations is the Sierra Club, 1050 Mills Tower, San Francisco, California 94105. It has chapters all over the Western United States, but you'll also find chapters in the Midwest and East. The club goes back to 1892 and its aims are simple:

> . . . *to help people* explore, enjoy, and protect parks, wilderness, waters, forests, and wildlife.
> . . . *to rescue places* that made America beautiful and can keep it beautiful.

A junior (ages twelve to twenty-one) only pays $3.50 to

join the Sierra Club, which has trips and camps of every kind. As one Sierra Club member puts it: "The sky is your roof, the ground your bed, and all the rooms are air-conditioned on Sierra Club outings." Club trips are *wilderness* outings designed to take people not to tourist spots, but into the wilderness where there are only trails, into the wild, virgin country where one finds deep quietness, wild creatures, streams, meadows, and forests as they have evolved over thousands of years, untouched and unchanged by man.

Each year the Club Outing Committee schedules over a hundred such wilderness outings. They may range from a week of family camping close to home to a six-week expedition to the Alps, from a leisurely float trip down the Yampa River to a strenuous backpack trip over twelve-thousand-foot passes. Outings are normally in summer, although there have been spring trips to the desert wilderness of the Southwest and elsewhere. Most of the trips are in the West because that is where most wilderness is; but there are also trips down the rivers of Maine and Ontario and into the Adirondacks and the Appalachians for the members in the East.

Outings vary in size (from twenty to over fifty people), in distance covered, and in physical exertion demanded. Many trips welcome novices; a few are for experienced mountaineers only. Participants have ranged in age from one year to over eighty.

On Sierra Club outings you agree to these rules: (1) you accept the leader's decisions and instructions; (2) you may not wander off alone; (3) *with the leader's permission* you may do anything reasonable—try a different route, climb a peak, explore—as long as he knows exactly where you are going and as long as he thinks you are up to it.

The Sierra Club also arranges trail maintenance parties for fellows and girls (minimum age fifteen) who have large quantities of energy and who enjoy working hard. Work includes leveling of mountain paths, fighting erosion, and other trail chores. But there is plenty of time to hike, climb, swim.

If you live in California, and are rugged enough for one-week high-altitude programs, you should also know about the Mountaineering Guide Service in Big Pine (Box 327, Big Pine, California 93513). Here's a group of top guides who introduce novices to mountaineering, provide a refresher course for once-a-season climbers, and improve skills of experienced climbers. The ratio of instructors to students is about one to four, so you get lots of personal attention. Teen-agers can come if they bring parents, who can just watch from camp. Most of the climbers are adults who have done a lot of backpacking and don't mind moving in twelve-thousand- and fourteen-thousand-foot altitudes, so you've got to be in shape. The guide service has no objection to girl students.

The Mountaineers (Box 122, Seattle, Washington 98111) is a well-established club that has been taking girls and boys of all ages on hiking and climbing trips for more than sixty years. Outings range from afternoon hikes to expeditions lasting several weeks. Most of these are free, except a few of the longer trips on which professional packers or cooks are employed. Throughout the year there are short easy hikes scheduled every weekend. During the winter and spring months there are snowshoe trips. Many of the hikes and snowshoe trips are "beginner's specials." If you want to learn actual climbing you are encouraged to take one of the climbing courses which start early each spring. Courses consist of several lectures, practice sessions in mountain areas, and many "experience" climbs. The Mountaineers' school is famous for turning out good rock climbers. (Cost is minimal.)

In the Pacific Northwest, The Mount Rainier Guide

Service (1525 11th Avenue, Seattle, Washington 98122) teaches as well as guides. Your outdoor school will be on Mount Rainier. (The rest of the family can vacation at the Paradise Inn.) Mount Rainier was the training ground of the American Mount Everest Expedition, and it offers challenges for the expert as well as the beginner. Every year, hundreds of people come from all over the country to climb this great mountain and use the experienced personnel of the Mount Rainier Guide Service.

Experienced guides take groups to the summit of Mount Rainier three times a week, from June 10 until September 5. The climb requires two days with one night at high camp. (Guide fee is thirty-two dollars per person.) Or try a climbing seminar—five days of instruction, practice, discussion, and fun on the slopes of Mount Rainier including a climb to the summit. (The cost of ninety-five dollars includes food.) In addition, rock-climbing, snow-climbing, and ice-climbing classes are held daily through the summer. At least one snow-climbing class is recommended before the summit climb.

Still another Seattle-based school is the Rocky Mountain Guide Service and Mountaineering School, Inc., 4725 30th Avenue, N.E., Seattle, Washington 98108.

A mountaineering course—it needn't last longer than one to three days—is recommended for all beginners. Even if you have an experienced friend, you get ahead faster by taking a course. The friend with experience will be only too happy if you *already* know the basic principles, for he will then be able to take you on more interesting climbs.

Mountaineering schools train climbers well. Rock technique, ice technique, rope management, the use of pitons, glacier precautions, rescue techniques, and first aid are all taught. The various sources of danger on mountains are

Mountaineering students get their
first talk about climbing. (*Public Service Co.*)

usually touched on. Compass- and map-reading are soon made familiar to you, and your instructors will also talk to you about meteorology, geology, and botany.

What sort of skills must American and Canadian mountaineering instructors have? What rules must they live by? The instructor is usually an expert climber himself. He must be able to tie all knots used in rock climbing and mountaineering. He must have a knowledge of all safety factors and must possess superior knowledge of climbing techniques. The instructor must be personally capable of the most difficult technical climbs, have a good safety record, and have *three or more* years of actual climbing experience. Of course, the instructor must be genuinely interested in the safety and instruction of all his students.

One of the schools which lives by all these rules is the Exum School of American Mountaineering (Moose Post Office, Moose, Wyoming 83012). In the Grand Tetons, this school employs only the foremost teachers. (Four of them were on the American Mount Everest Expedition.) All summer long, the Exum School gives beginner, intermediate, and advanced classes. A number of girls also enroll in the mountaineering school and climb the Tetons. The cost is about ten dollars per day. After learning to climb, you're allowed to join an ascent of the Grand Teton. The minimum age of all students is fourteen, although occasionally younger (but sturdy) boys have been taken on also.

The Barry Corbet Climbing School (Box 477, Jackson, Wyoming 83001) is newer, but operates in the same magnificent mountains. Boys of eight and up can learn backpacking here, and anyone over fourteen may register for one-day classes in all phases of rock climbing and mountaineering. You don't need experience here, just the willingness to try. Bring good boots, gloves, a lunch, and warm clothes (the Tetons can get miserably cold and wet even in midsummer). The beginners program includes basic instruction in mountaineering equipment, knots, pace, and belaying. The class will climb several moderate rock pitches and have a chance to practice belaying under realistic conditions. Classes are small and the fee is twelve dollars.

As an "intermediate" you go deeper into knots, learn the causes of belay failure, discuss mountain hazards, and are taught high-anglerock climbing and piton placements and long rappels. "Advanced" climbing school here means more knots, more advanced belaying techniques, discussion of party leadership, difficult high-angle climbing, artificial climbing, piton placement, rescue technique. (The fee is twenty dollars.)

In Wyoming you can take part in an even more unique (but much longer) adventure. This is the National Outdoor Leadership School (Box 779, Lander, Wyoming 82520). Call it NOLS, for short. The NOLS has a six-week course for young men thirteen, fourteen, and fifteen years of age. The course includes a month-long expedition into the Wind River Range of Wyoming. Here, in the thousands of square miles of wild country, you find large snow fields and glaciers. There are more than a thousand lakes for trout fishing, hundreds of miles of wild canyons and peaks for mountain climbing, primitive forests full of wildlife. The NOLS includes instruction in leadership, organization, supply, equipment, logistics, mountaineering, rock climbing, glacier and snow techniques, rescue, first aid, survival, accident prevention, fishing, rations, cooking, map reading, horsemanship, forest-fire fighting, safety, advanced camping techniques, and practical conservation. The complete isolation (during the six weeks there is no contact with the outside world, not even a jeep road) is a real experience. The school costs several hundred dollars. And remember: NOLS isn't for sissies.

If you prefer an easier summer camp in the west, consider Sun Valley, Idaho. Here High Wilderness Camp offers two ten-day sessions in the Pioneer Mountains east of Sun Valley. The first five days are devoted to climbing instruction. The balance of the session includes exploration of the back country, and backpacking in the land of no trails. First session, boys ages twelve to fourteen, every July. Second session, boys fifteen to seventeen, in August. Prices are high.

The Canadian Mountain Holidays Camp (Box 583, Banff, Alberta) employs excellent instructors and guides. Every year, these experts teach youngsters from the ages of twelve to seventeen during a special "Junior Mountaineering Week." The camp is usually at Lake O'Hara in the Yoho National Park, British Columbia. Parents can stay at a nearby lodge.

The Alpine Club of Canada (P.O. Box 1265, Calgary, Alberta) has camps and seminars of every kind. The club doesn't have to make a profit, so charges are reasonable. Several five-day camps are also organized by the Skyline Trail Hikers of the Canadian Rockies (622 Madison Avenue, Calgary, Alberta). Hiking and camping only. You must be eighteen years old, or if you're younger, parents, a bigger brother, or friends must be along.

There is no such regulation for the famous Outward Bound Schools. *No* relatives can be on hand when you get your first taste of battling nature here.

The four schools are run pretty much along the same lines. They are anything but easy. Take the Colorado Outward Bound School, for instance. Its location at Marble, Colorado (Zip code 81623), is in remote rugged country. You're at 8,800 feet on the western slopes of the Rocky Mountains, 230 miles from Denver and 70 miles from Aspen. The school is two miles on a jeep road above Marble, a small ghost town. The twenty-six–day program gives boys from all walks of life the chance, under guidance, to face danger, hardship, and even loneliness. It's a place where, through learning the skills

A MOUNTAINEERING SCHOOL includes actual climbs—the best way to learn. (*U.S. Air Force Academy*)

of fire fighting, mountain climbing, and survival, a boy begins to understand more about his own abilities and limitations than he has ever known before.

Anyone who has tried an Outward Bound experience once wouldn't do it again voluntarily. It's that rugged! For instance, you have to run a mile at dawn. Then you plunge into an icy mountain stream. You have to scale high walls. You even have to inch along a two-hundred-foot rope strung thirty feet above the ground! Outward Bounders also do much mountain walking, backpacking, and high-altitude camping, and they get instruction in the rappel. The most important event of each course is called the "solo." Each boy is led to an uninhabited, primitive area. There he must stay for three days and three nights. Equipment is minimal—a bit of line and a hook, a sleeping bag, eight matches, a nine-foot-square plastic sheet, a first-aid kit, two quarts of water, and a knife. Each student faces the test of survival. His food supply depends on his skill and his knowledge of edible plant and animal life. The "solo" is a test of boy against the wilderness.

Apart from the Colorado school, there are Outward Bound Schools in Oregon (at McKenzie Bridge, 97401), where you do a lot of ice climbing, in Ely, Minnesota 55731 (severe wilderness training), in Andover, Massachusetts 01810, and on Hurricane Island, Maine 04863 (here, in addition to cliff scaling, you do some sailing).

All the Outward Bound outposts are nonprofit, so the fees are very low. Contributions allow the schools to take needy young men totally free. Several Outward Bound places have special weeks for girls, who must be just as fit as the boys. A lot of the boys come from big cities, and the school takes on anyone strong enough, and never mind race, religion, or national origin. All are equal here.

If you only have time on weekends, and happen to live in

Colorado, you should take a look at the programs of the Colorado Mountain Club (1723 East 16th Avenue, Denver 80218). Juniors (ages twelve and up) pay only three dollars a year. Every weekend, there are hikes, climbs, camping trips. You don't have to be a member to come along as a guest. An excellent club activity is the Mountaineering Seminar (small charge), where very patient volunteer-instructors teach you. You hear lectures about first aid, safety, and whatever else you'd like to know about rock climbing.

Where do you find hiking companions in the East? One of the best organized and most important groups is the Appalachian Mountain Club. With a membership of twelve thousand, this club is able to maintain its own huts in New England. They have many summer camps and outdoor activities. The membership fee is only three dollars for anyone under nineteen. The club's aims and services are:

- The building and maintenance of trails, huts, and shelters.
- The publication of important material—scientific, historical, and cultural—on the mountains of New England and nearby regions, including guidebooks and maps.
- An extensive mountaineering library in New England, available for use by all interested persons.
- The training of beginners in hiking, camping, rock climbing, skiing, mountaineering, white-water canoeing, and other outdoor sports.
- The teaching of the proper safety precautions for mountaineers and hikers, and the organization of rescue parties for those in trouble.
- The conservation of natural resources and the preservation of the wilderness.
- The presentation of public lectures on important

events and discoveries in the fields of climbing, mountaineering, exploration, science, geology, glaciology, and natural history.

Information on membership and application blanks, as well as folders on the club huts and camps, can be obtained by writing to the Appalachian Mountain Club, 5 Joy Street Boston, Massachusetts 02108.

If you live anywhere in New York State (including Albany, Ithaca, Keene, Keene Valley, Lake Placid, New York City, Plattsburgh, Poughkeepsie, Saranac Lake, Schenectady, and Syracuse) you should get acquainted with the Adirondack Mountain Club, Gabriels, New York 12939. Its 2,500 members do interesting things like trooping up trailless Catskills Peaks (with map and compass), hiking up other four-thousand-foot-high peaks, and rock climbing.

Remember, too, that wherever you may live in North America, YWCA's, social clubs, YMCA's, school recreation departments, and a few churches may include rock-climbing lessons in their summer programs.

Other useful addresses for further information are Wilderness Society, 2144 P Street, N.W., Washington, D.C. 20005; American Forestry Association, 919 17th Street, N.W., Washington, D.C. 20006; and Bureau of Outdoor Recreation, Department of the Interior, Washington, D.C. 20240.

Good hiking! Good climbing!

12   mountain manners:
a few dos and don'ts

If you use the wilderness properly, the person who follows in your footsteps will never know you were there, and he will enjoy his trip as much as you did. Keep him in mind as you travel through the wilderness. *Take nothing but pictures; leave nothing but footprints.*

• Bury foil wrap. The food traces and odors attract wild animals. Instant snapshot film is poisonous to the creatures of the forest.

• Leaving a dirty camp is inexcusable. Make it your responsibility to leave it spotless. Burn trash and pack out the cans, glass, foil, and other unburnables. *Bury human wastes.* (A garden trowel will help with this "kitty-cat" method of waste disposal.)

• Soap or detergents should not be put into streams or lakes because of the harm they do to aquatic life. Try to dispose of wash water in a rocky area where drainage will not reach nearby plants.

• Only fools paint rocks or carve their names into trees.

• At lower altitudes you may find gates of barbed wire or old wooden boards across the trail. These limit or control the movement of animals put there to pasture. Leave any gate as you find it, open or closed.

• Building trails is expensive. Erosion caused by hikers who save time by cutting "switchbacks" and taking other shortcuts can be very destructive.

• Flowers, ferns, and shrubs should not be picked. Leave them for others to enjoy.

• The campfire is a friend to man when he uses it carefully. It will keep him warm, cook his food, dry his clothes, and even add a flickering light of friendship to night's dark shadows.

Most people are careful with campfires. They follow state and local fire laws. They build their fires in the right places and at the right times, keep them small, and put them out before they leave. If everyone were that careful, campfires would not start forest fires.

An unattended campfire or a spark from a too-large fire can cause an entire forest to burn. Fire damages watersheds, destroys timber, and blackens recreation areas. It kills forest animals and often leads to serious erosion damage.

So when building a fire, clear the fire area of grass, needles, and other flammable material. Circle the fire with rocks, and make sure there is a cleared area four feet in diameter around the rocks. Keep your fire *small*. Never build it against trees or logs, or near brush.

Never break camp until your fire is out, *dead* out. Stir the coals while soaking them with water, turn burned sticks and drench both sides. Then douse again. Wet the ground around the fire and be sure the last spark is dead. Never build bonfires or burn slash or brush in *windy* weather or while there is the slightest danger that the fire will get away. Remember: water kills a fire—dirt only slows it down. Douse it—don't bury it.

• Chain saws and motorcycles are noisy. Motorized equipment of any sort has no place in the wilderness.

For more information about mountain manners, here are some addresses for useful free pamphlets, brochures, booklets:

American Forestry Association, 919 17th Street, N.W., Washington, D.C. 20006

The Conservation Foundation, 1250 Connecticut Avenue, N.W., Washington, D.C. 20036

Good Outdoor Manners Association, P.O. Box 7095, Seattle, Washington 98133

The Izaak Walton League of America, 1326 Waukegan Road, Glenview, Illinois 60025

Keep America Beautiful, Inc., 99 Park Avenue, New York, New York 10016

National Audubon Society, 1130 Fifth Avenue, New York, New York 10028

National Parks Association, 1300 New Hampshire Avenue, N.W., Washington, D.C. 20036

National Recreation and Park Association, 1700 Pennsylvania Ave., N.W., Washington, D.C. 20006

National Trust for Historic Preservation, Decatur House, 748 Jackson Place, N.W., Washington, D.C. 20006

The Nature Conservancy, 1522 K Street, N.W., Washington, D.C. 20005

Sierra Club, Mills Tower, San Francisco, California 94104

The Wilderness Society, 729 15th Street, N.W., Washington, D.C. 20005

Wildlife Management Institute, Wire Building, Washington, D.C. 20005

glossary:

mountaineering terms

ANCHOR ROPE: The part of a climbing rope tied from a belayer to a nearby anchor point. It holds the belayer firmly in his belay position in case of a fall by the climber.

AVALANCHE: The fall or sliding of a mass of snow and ice, often dislodging earth and rocks, down a mountain slope.

BALANCE CLIMBING: Movement up cliffs and slopes too steep for walking.

BELAYING: The playing, paying out and taking in, of a rope tied to a climber and running around the body of a belayer or around a tree, rock, or through a snaplink. This term also includes the application of braking action on the rope by the belayer in order to prevent a fall by the climber from becoming serious.

BELAY POINT: The point selected and used by the belayer from which he can best protect a climber and himself from a fall. Also a tree, rock, piton, or other object which may be used for the purpose of belaying.

CARABINER (SNAP LINK): An oval metal ring with a hinged section, the gate, which can be linked to a solid object while letting the rope run through itself freely.

CHIMNEY: A vertical opening large enough for the body of a climber.

CHOCKSTONE: A stone which has become wedged in a chimney tending to block it.

CHUTE: An opening caused by erosion or glacial action, vertical or sloping, and generally wider than a chimney.

CLIFF: a high, steep face.

CONTINUOUS CLIMBING: Climbing in which two or more people, connected by a rope, move up a large cliff in a series of leads (distances of less than a rope length). Some people use "continuous climbing" to mean all the climbers moving at the same time.

CORNICE: The mass of snow overhanging the side of a ridge.

CRAMPONS: Metal frames which are attached to shoes or boots by straps and from which spikes project downward to allow walking on ice or hard snow.

CREVASSE: An openng in the surface of a glacier.

EXPOSED CLIMB: A climb from which a fall would be dangerous.

FACE: A sheer unbroken vertical front such as a cliff.

FIXED ROPE: A rope secured to a steep slope or cliff by pitons, rocks, trees, used as a handline to aid climbers in ascending and descending.

FREE CLIMBING: Climbing without the aid of ropes.

GLACIERS: Large, slowly moving masses of ice and snow in the valleys of high mountains.

GLISSADING: Descending a snow slope by sliding on the feet in a standing position without the use of skis.

GULLY: A narrow ravine formed by erosion.

HOLD: Hand or foot support on rock.

ICE AX: An instrument similar to a pick consisting of a wooden shaft with a point on one end and a head consisting of a pick and blade on the other. Intended primarily for cutting holds in snow and ice, as an aid to balance, and in probing for crevasses.

LEADER: The first man and the man in charge. The first man in the party in upward climbs, belayed from below.

MOUNTAIN WALKING: Various methods of crossing rocky terrain on foot.

PARTY CLIMB: Several men roped together to climb a cliff.

PITCH: A steep and difficult part of a mountain where it is impractical or impossible to find a belay position.

PITON: An iron spike used as an aid in climbing. It is hammered into cracks in the rock and serves as a belay point or anchor.

PITON HAMMER: A short, light hammer used for driving pitons. It has a wooden handle and one side of the head comes to a sharp point which is used primarily for clearing debris from cracks.

RAPPEL: The process whereby a climber slides down a rope to lower himself down steep slopes or rock.

RAPPEL POINT: The rock, tree, or rope sling to which the rappel rope is secured.

RIB: A small ridge on a rock face.

SCREE: Slopes composed of small rocks and gravel varying in size from sand to pieces about the size of a man's fist.

SNAP LINK: An oval-shaped metal ring with a hinged gate which permits fastening it to a rope or piton. See CARABINER.

STATIC CLIMBING: Climbing on a cliff, one rope length or less in height, where the belayer is always above the climber.

TENSION CLIMBING: Climbing in which the belayer holds the climber on the rock with tension, through pitons, on the climbing rope.

TIMBERLINE: The line at which trees cease to grow. The altitude depends on wind, moisture, soil conditions, and geographical location.

TRAIL MARKERS: Wooden markers placed at intervals along a route to identify it in fog, storm, or when the trail has become obliterated. Also used are sticks, willow wands, branches, rocks, and blazed trees.

TRAVERSING: Moving across or in a zigzag pattern, rather than directly up or down.

WALL: Another term used for cliff or face.

bibliography: some books

Hiking and Camping

Brief Guide to Hiking, D. Deer
   Preston Publications, Atlanta, Ga., 1968

Catskill Trails, W. D. Mulholland
   State of New York Conservation Dept., Albany, 1967

Complete Book of Camping, Maurice Decker and Leonard Miracle
   Harper & Row, New York, 1961

Golden Guide to Camping, Robert E. Smallman
   Golden Press, New York, 1965

Hiking
   Boy Scouts of America, New Brunswick, N.J., 1962

Lightweight Equipment for Hiking, Camping and Mountaineering
   Potomac Appalachian Trail Club, Washington, D.C., 1966

The Long Trail
   Green Mountain Club, Rutland, Vt., 1966

The Magic of Walking, Aaron Sussman and Ruth Goode
Simon & Schuster, New York, 1968

The Man Who Walked through Time, Colin Fletcher
Knopf, New York, 1967

Nelson's Encyclopedia of Camping, E. C. Barnes
Thomas Nelson and Sons, New York, 1963

Mountaineering

All about Mountains and Mountaineering, Anne Terry
White
Random House, New York, 1962

Americans on Everest, James Ramsey Ullman
Lippincott, Philadelphia, 1964

Basic Mountaineering, edited by Henry Mandolf
Sierra Club, San Diego, Calif., 1965

Climber's Guide to the Tetons, Leigh Ortenburger
Sierra Club, San Francisco, 1956

Direttissima: The Eiger Assault, Peter Gillman and Dou-
gal Haston
Harper & Row, New York, 1966

Everest Diary, Lute Jerstad and J. D. McCallum
Follett, Chicago, 1966

Four against Everest, Woodrow Wilson Sayre
Prentice-Hall, Englewood Cliffs, N.J., 1964

Fundamentals of Rock Climbing, Advance Rock Climbing Committee
MIT Outing Club, Cambridge, Mass. 02139, 1968

Guide to the Colorado Mountains, Robert Ormes
Swallow, Chicago, 1966

The Mountaineering Handbook, Curtis Casewit and Dick
  Pownall
  Lippincott, Philadelphia, 1968

Mountaineering: The Freedom of the Hills, The Mountaineers
  The Mountaineers, Seattle, Wash. 98111, 1960

The Mountain of My Fear, David Roberts
  Vanguard, New York, 1968

Mountain Rescue Techniques, Wastl Mariner
  The Mountaineers, Seattle, Wash. 98111, 1968

Straight Up, James Ramsey Ullman
  Doubleday, Garden City, N.Y., 1968

Various Books

Anyone Can Backpack in Comfort, James Ralph Johnson
  McKay, New York, 1965

Earth Science, Richard Pearl
  Grosset & Dunlap, New York, 1964

First Aid Textbook, American Red Cross
  Doubleday, Garden City, N.Y.

First Aid Textbook for Juniors, American Red Cross
  Doubleday, Garden City, N.Y.

Food for Knapsackers and Other Trail Travelers, Winnie
  Thomas and Hasse Bunnelle
  Sierra Club, San Francisco, 1966

Going Light—With Backpack on Burro, David Brower
  Sierra Club, San Francisco, 1956

The Handbook of Wilderness Travel, George and Iris
  Wells

Colorado Outdoor Sports, Box 5544, Denver, 80217, 1968

How to Know the Minerals and Rocks, Richard Pearl
New American Library, New York, 1963

Living off the Country, Bradford Angier
Stackpole, Harrisburg, Pa., 1956

Mountain Men of the Early West, Olive W. Burt
Hawthorn, New York, 1967

The National Parks of America, Stewart L. Udall and
Editors of Country Beautiful
G. P. Putnam, New York, 1966

The Outdoor Encyclopedia, Ted Kesting
A. S. Barnes & Company, New York, 1957

Ski Fever, Curtis Casewit
Hawthorn, New York, 1965

Ski Racing: Advice by the Experts, Curtis W. Casewit
Arco, New York, 1969

The State Parks, Tilden Freeman
Knopf, New York, 1962

Thirty Hikes in Alaska
The Mountaineers, Seattle, Wash., 1967